Robert O'Neill
& Martin Shovel
with Barry Tomalin

Cartoons by Lo Cole
& Martin Shovel

Classroom Edition

BBC English

Published by BBC English 1989

BBC English, PO Box 76,
Bush House, London WC2B 4PH
Self-study bilingual version first published 1988
(Japanese edition) by BBC English and ILS (Japan) Ltd

Editing: Stenton Associates
Design: Ken Vail Graphic Design/Jim Wire
Cover photograph (background): ZEFA
Typesetting: Goodfellow and Egan/Ace Filmsetting Ltd
Printing: Scotprint Ltd

The Lost Secret course components
Study sets

PAL VHS	1 85497 134 4
PAL Betamax	1 85497 135 2
NTSC VHS	1 85497 136 0
NTSC Betamax	1 85497 137 9
Classroom Book	**1 85497 133 6**
Teachers' Book	1 85497 138 7
Bilingual Japanese book	1 85497 131 X
Bilingual German book	1 85497 132 8
Bilingual Spanish book	1 85497 182 4

Contents

To the Teacher

Welcome to **The Lost Secret**, a compelling video adventure for 'false beginners' and learners at elementary level and above.

This book accompanies the video, which is just over two and a quarter hours long. The book is divided into eleven units corresponding to the eleven episodes of the video. Working through the book will provide up to fifty-five hours of classroom teaching.

There is also a *Teachers' Book* which you should obtain. The *Teachers' Book* gives detailed suggestions on how to exploit the video fully with your class or group. It includes an analysis of vocabulary and grammar; ideas for classroom activities such as pairwork, role plays and discussions; varied techniques for showing the video; and a complete set of scripts.

The video itself is time-coded for ease of use. The time code will allow you to find your place in the video very quickly and will also help you to relate the activities in this book and in the *Teachers' Book* to the appropriate point on the video.

Using video is not just a motivating way of presenting new language. It is also an exciting method of teaching which will improve the way your students learn English. Whether you are experienced or inexperienced in using video, this book, together with the *Teachers' Book*, will show you how to proceed, what you can expect to achieve and how best to achieve it.

How this book works

Stage 1: Preview The first page of each unit helps you to prepare your group for some of the new language used in the episode. It also refers to some of the main events – but without spoiling the suspense. Many of the Preview pages also include questions on the story so far.

Stage 2: The whole episode The second page of the unit gives the class the chance to watch the whole episode and to answer some general comprehension questions, before going on to look at the scenes in more detail.

Stage 3: Scene by scene From the third page onwards, the episode is broken up into sections or scenes which are studied in detail. The class watches the section indicated by the time codes and completes a series of exercises. Strip cartoons are used to present important scenes from the video. Later in the book, 'novelisations' – short texts from the story – begin to take over. The cartoons, exercises and novelisations together contain almost the whole video script, and provide a record of the story which is useful for reference and for follow-up work after viewing.

Stage 4: Focuses Each unit contains two pages of Focus exercises which highlight key structures or vocabulary from the episode. The exercises are illustrated with cartoons which help to make the language points easier to understand.

Stage 5: Review The final page of each unit provides an opportunity to look back over the events and the language of the episode. It usually contains a story summary exercise, extra language work, speculation about the next episode and a short test.

At the end of the book is a selective summary of some of the most important grammar points from the course.

The Lost Secret covers the main structural items in the Council of Europe's Waystage syllabus. It does so in the context of an exciting story. Good luck with your investigation of **The Lost Secret**!

Unit 1

THE BEGINNING

This is a story about

a beautiful woman

a doctor

a man without a name

a strange plant

a mysterious professor

and several other people.

THE LOST SECRET

Preview

1 Look at the picture. Find the words.

river fish bird ticket man woman bridge train

2 Look at the questions (1–6). Find good answers (a–f).

1 How much is that?
2 Where's your ticket?
3 What are you doing?
4 Is this the train to London?
5 What's wrong?
6 Can you speak English?

a) It's here.
b) Yes, a little.
c) It's 50 pence.
d) I'm leaving. Goodbye.
e) No, it's going to Oxford.
f) I can't find my ticket.

3 Can you understand these phrases from episode 1? Which one is strange?

00:00
12:15

Now watch episode 1 (00:00–12:15) . Don't try to understand every word.

Exercise 1

Look at this cartoon from the video. Where do the sentences (a–d) go? Put the letters in the answer box below.

a) Yes, I am going to Winchester. **b**) Coffee? **c**) Thank you. **d**) The train is leaving!

2:16
3:55

Now watch this part again. Listen and check your answers.

Answer box

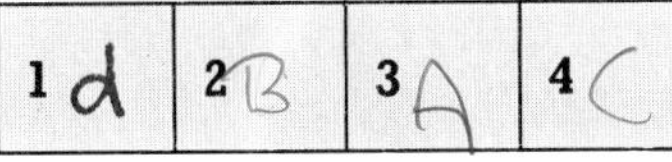

3:56
6:50

Now watch this part again.

Exercise 2

Look at the cartoon strip. Where do these words (a–i) go?

a) much **b)** you **c)** your **d)** is **e)** my **f)** change **g)** sandwich **h)** I **i)** sorry

1	2	3	4	5	6	7	8	9

6:51
9:06

Watch this part again.

Exercise 3

Look at the cartoon strip. Where do these sentences (a–e) go?

a) Stop that! Come on!
b) What's he doing?
c) There!
d) She's going, George.
e) I'm going.

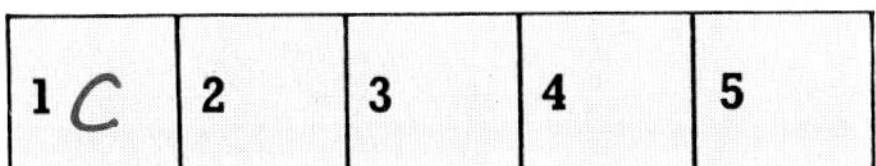

1	2	3	4	5

9:07
12:15

Watch this part again.

Exercise 4

What are they saying: **a**) or **b**)?

1 **a**) Where are you?
b) What are you?

2 **a**) Are you a fish? Can you swim?
b) Are you a bird? Can you fly?

3 **a**) Well? What are they doing now, Alice?
b) Well? What are you doing now, Alice?

4 **a**) He's talking.
b) She's talking.

5 **a**) No! Don't do it! Don't jump!
b) Yes! Do it! Jump!

1 b	2	3	4	5

Exercise 5

Which sentence (a–h) goes with which picture (1–8)?

a) This is a bird. It can fly.
b) This is a dog. A dog can't fly.
c) This isn't a bird or a dog. It's a fish. Fish can swim.
d) And this is a cat.
e) This is a plane. It's flying to London.
f) And this is a train. It's going to London too.
g) This is a car. It's in London.
h) This isn't a car or a train. It's a bus. It's in London too.

1 d	2	3	4	5	6	7	8

Exercise 6

What are the four missing words?

Are you __1__ to Winchester?
Yes, __2__ am.
Can I see your __3__, please?
Here you are.
__4__ you.

a) ticket **b**) I **c**) Thank **d**) going

1 d	2	3	4

Focus One

Where is/are ______ going?

Find the right question for each picture.
The questions are in the box below.

a) Where are you going?
b) Where is it going?
c) Where is she going?
d) Where is he going?

1 C	**2**	**3**	**4**

Focus Two

her/his/my/your

Find the missing word. Is it **a)** *her*, **b)** *his*, **c)** *my* or **d)** *your* sandwich?

1 b	**2**	**3**	**4**

Focus Three

this/that
one packet/two packets
How much is it?/How much are they?

Find the right sentence for each picture.
The sentences are in the box below.

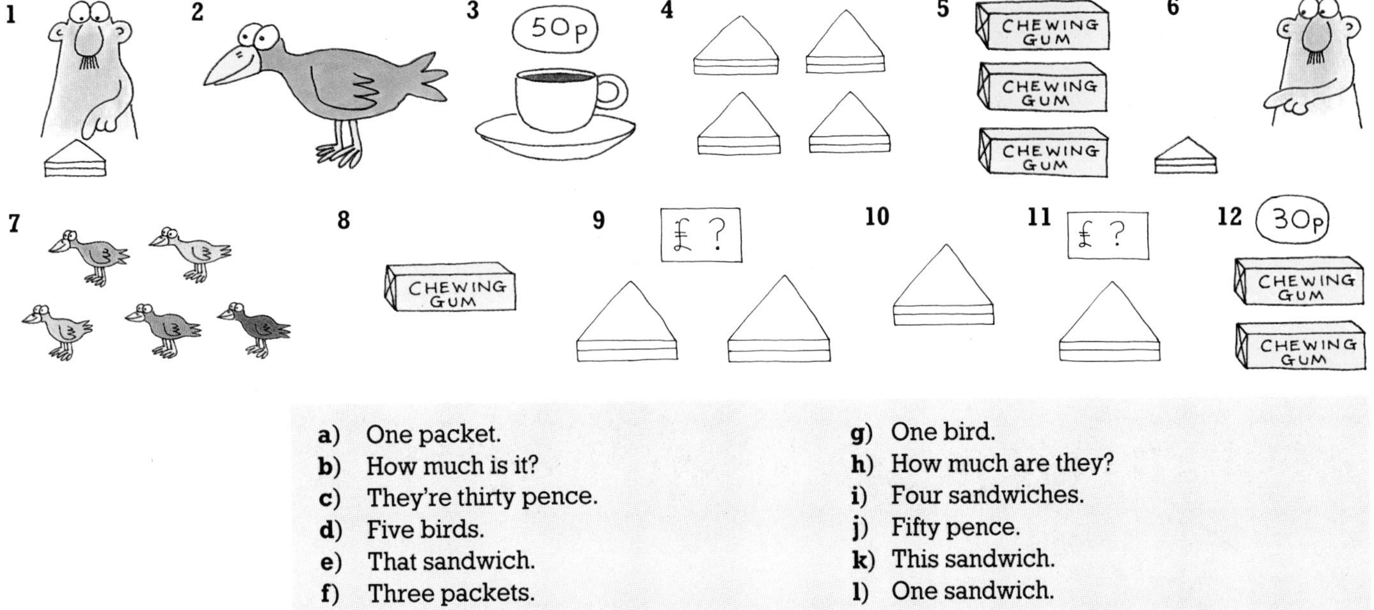

a) One packet.
b) How much is it?
c) They're thirty pence.
d) Five birds.
e) That sandwich.
f) Three packets.
g) One bird.
h) How much are they?
i) Four sandwiches.
j) Fifty pence.
k) This sandwich.
l) One sandwich.

1 k	2	3	4	5	6	7	8	9	10	11	12

Focus Four

What are you/they doing?
I'm/We're/They're ______ ing.

Find the right answer to each question.
The answers are in the box below.

a) They're going.
b) I'm watching television.
c) We're swimming.
d) They're talking.

1 b	2	3	4

Unit 1

Review

1 Read about episode 1. Find the wrong sentences.

1 A man is on a bridge.
2 He is saying, 'I'm a fish. I can swim.'

3 They are on a bus.
4 They are going to Winchester.

5 The woman can't find her ticket.

6 The woman is saying, 'I'm sorry. Very sorry. I'm going.'

7 The man is saying, 'Remember. You're a bird! You can fly!

8 The woman is saying, 'Go on! Jump!'

2 Find the missing word. Is it *am*, *is* or *are*?

1 What ____________ you doing?
2 The train ____________ going to London.
3 My name ____________ George.
4 I ____________ from Liverpool.
5 Where ____________ my tickets?
6 Where ____________ my ticket?
7 How much ____________ this sandwich?
8 How much ____________ these sandwiches?

Unit 2

WHO IS HE?

Preview

1 Do you know?

1 What is he saying?
2 What is wrong with him?
3 Where is he?

2 People say these things (1–6) in episode 2. Find good answers (a–f).

1 Would you like a cup of tea?	**a)** Thirteen.
2 What's your name?	**b)** Yes, please.
3 Where do you live?	**c)** No, I'm an American.
4 Has he got any identification?	**d)** Janet Black.
5 What's six and seven?	**e)** Yes, here is his passport.
6 Are you English?	**f)** In London.

3 Study these words from episode 2.

questions hospital busy colour listen remember memory perhaps

Now use the words in these sentences.

1 Would you like to ________ to the radio?
2 I'm sorry, but I can't see you today. I'm very ________ .
3 I can't see you this morning, but ________ I can see you this afternoon.
4 Can I ask you some ________ ?
5 I can't ________ your telephone number. Can you give it to me again, please?
6 This man is very ill. Take him to the ________ .
7 He doesn't know his name or address. There's something wrong with his ________ .
8 What ________ are her eyes? Blue or brown?

4 Can you understand these sentences from episode 2?

Excuse me, sir, but I think he's ill.

Thank you for the appointment. I know you're busy, but I think it's important.

I'm a doctor. Perhaps I can help you.

'To Sabina, with love, Basil.'

12:26
24:50

Watch episode 2. Don't try to understand every word. Then do exercise 1.

Exercise 1

Look at the pictures (1–6). Find the sentence (a–f) that goes with each picture.

a) This woman is a policewoman. She has got the man's jacket.
b) This woman is a secretary. She is in Dr Roberts' office and she is saying 'Who's calling, please?'
c) There is something wrong with this man's memory. He can't remember his name. He can't remember his address. He can't remember anything!
d) The man in this picture is Inspector Marvin. He is asking the man some questions but the man can't answer them. The other man in the picture is a policeman, too.
e) These things are all from the man's pockets. You can see a boarding card, a ticket, a pen and some matches.
f) The doctor is asking the man some questions too. She thinks she can help him. Inspector Marvin is listening.

1		2		3		4		5		6	

13:23
15:44

Now watch this part. Then do exercises 2 and 3.

Exercise 2

Read the cartoon strip. Then find the missing sentences (1–6) below (a–f).

How are you? How are you feeling? Are you cold? Here's your jacket.
What's wrong with him?
Would you like a cup of tea?
I'm...
Yes?
I'm a bird... I can fly.
You can what? 1
I don't know.
Inspector Marvin?
Yes. I'm Inspector Marvin. 2
Yes, sir.
Hello.
3
My name's Marvin. Inspector Marvin. Can I ask you some questions?
Questions?
Yes, questions. What's your name? Can you remember? 4
I don't know. I don't know my name.
Can you remember your address? 5
Where do you come from?
I can't remember.
He says he's a bird. He says he can fly.
A bird? What is your name?
6

a) Can you remember your name? **b**) What's wrong with him? **c**) Where do you live? **d**) I haven't got a name. **e**) Is that the man? **f**) Who are you?

Exercise 3

Find the sentences closest in meaning.

1 What's your address?
2 How are you?
3 Would you like a cup of tea?

a) Are you all right?
b) Can I get you a cup of tea?
c) Where do you live?

1	2	3

15:45
17:37

Now watch this part. Then do exercise 4.

Exercise 4

Find the six missing sentences here.

a) Any more questions, sir?
b) Yes. What about it?
c) Get me this number, please.
d) Just these things.
e) Has he got any identification?
f) No . . . wait a moment.

1	2	3	4	5	6

17:38
19:54

Now watch this part. Then do exercises 5, 6, 7 and 8.

Exercise 5

What does it mean: **a**), **b**) or **c**)?

1 appointment
a) something wrong with Mr Young
b) a time when he can see Dr Roberts
c) a telephone

2 busy
a) ill
b) in hospital
c) many things to do, people to see, etc

1	**2**

Exercise 6

True (T) or false (F)?

1 Mr Young can't come on Monday but he can come on Tuesday.
2 Dr Roberts is ill.
3 The secretary is ill.
4 Inspector Marvin is phoning Mr Young.
5 The inspector is phoning Dr Roberts.
6 Mr Young's next appointment is at three thirty next Tuesday.

1	**2**	**3**	**4**	**5**	**6**

Exercise 7

Read the dialogue and then find the missing words below.

Do you remember __1__? Inspector Marvin–David Marvin. Yes, that's right. There's a man here at the police station. Can you see __2__?

No, I'm sorry, I __3__. I'm busy today.

Yes, I know you're busy, but there's something wrong __4__ this man's memory. I think you can help him.

But Inspector, I'm very busy today.

Yes, I know, but this man can't remember anything. He can't remember __5__ name, he can't remember his address–he can't remember anything!

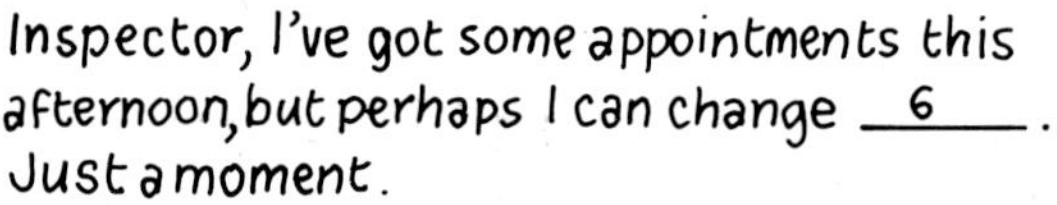

Hello Margaret, what __7__ my appointments this afternoon, please?

Well, __8__'s Mrs Gunn at two o'clock, and then there's Mr Sharp at three o'clock, so you're free at three thirty.

Thank you. Inspector? Can you come here, __9__ my clinic, at three thirty this afternoon? Good! Goodbye.

1	2	3	4	5	6	7	8	9
a) me	**a)** it	**a)** can	**a)** about	**a)** him	**a)** them	**a)** is	**a)** that	**a)** in
b) I	**b)** her	**b)** can't	**b)** in	**b)** her	**b)** her	**b)** are	**b)** here	**b)** to
c) my	**c)** him	**c)** don't	**c)** with	**c)** his	**c)** it	**c)** am	**c)** there	**c)** at

1	2	3	4	5	6	7	8	9

Exercise 8

What does it mean: **a)** or **b)**?

1 He can't remember anything.
a) He can remember one or two things.
b) He remembers nothing.

2 You're free at three thirty.
a) You have no appointments at three thirty.
b) You have one appointment at three thirty.

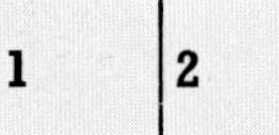

20:22
24:50

Now watch this part, and then do exercises 9 and 10.

Exercise 9

Find the missing parts of the dialogue.

a) Good. Now look at my eyes. What colour are they?
b) Good. And what's six and seven?
c) Good. Monday, Tuesday, Wednesday . . . go on.
d) Thank you for the appointment.
e) I'm not ill, am I?
f) Thirty.
g) How are you?
h) Please sit down.

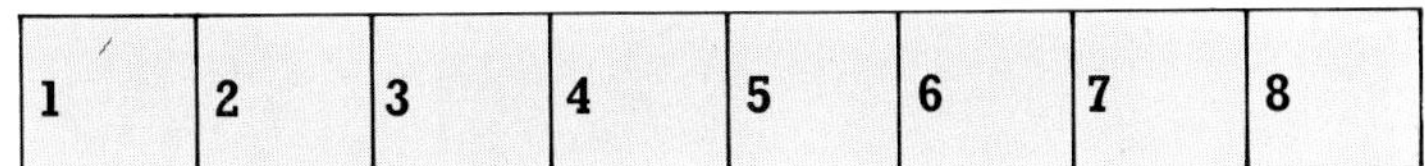

1	2	3	4	5	6	7	8

Exercise 10

Read the cartoon strip.

True (T) or false (F)?

1 He says he is English.
2 He knows his name but not his address.
3 There's nothing wrong with his memory.
4 He can remember a woman's name.
5 He says her name is Sabina.
6 He can answer the question 'What's six and seven?' but he can't answer the question 'What's your name?'

1	2	3	4	5	6

Exercise 11

Which word doesn't belong?

Example: one five sit nine

Answer: sit

1 Monday Friday Sunday England
2 clinic morning afternoon evening
3 policeman inspector doctor detective
4 sandwich moment second minute
5 blue red white beef
6 pen passport driving licence identification
7 look see watch talk
8 fish man cat bird

Write the words that don't belong here.

1 ________	5 ________
2 ________	6 ________
3 ________	7 ________
4 ________	8 ________

Exercise 12

Find the two strange sentences.

a) Please help me. It's very important.
b) Please help me. It isn't very important.
c) I know you're busy, but this isn't important.
d) I know you're busy, but this is important.

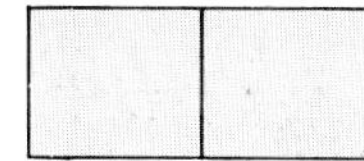

Exercise 13

Find the right words for the colours.

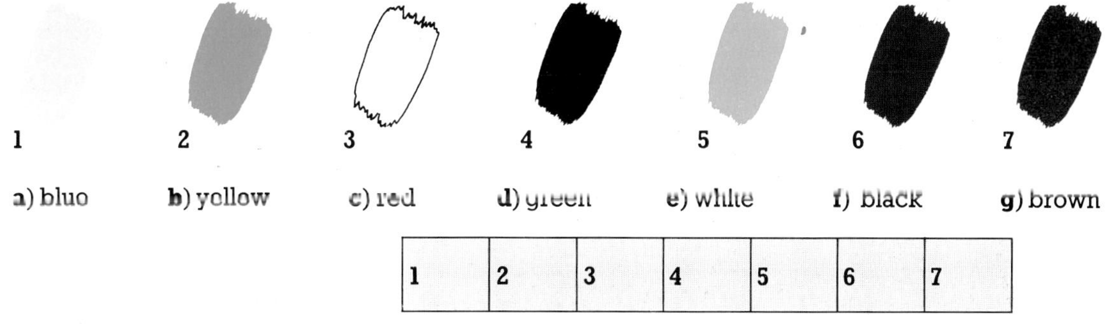

Exercise 14

Put the words for the numbers in the right order.

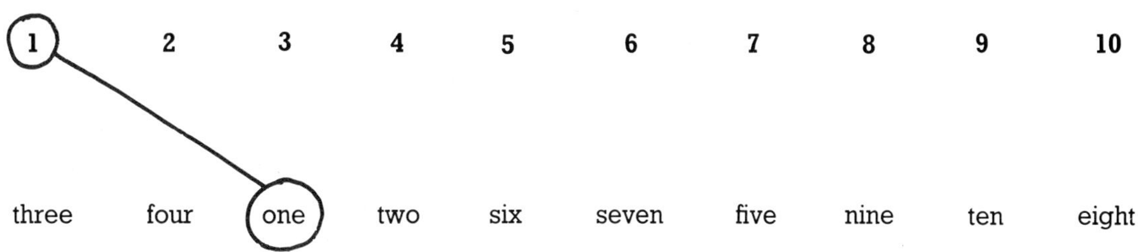

Focus One

Have you got ______?

Find the right questions for each picture. The questions are in the box below.

a) Have you got the time?
b) Have you got a cheese and tomato sandwich?
c) Have you got any fish?
d) Have you got a ticket?

1	**2**	**3**	**4**

Focus Two

It's ______ thirty.

What time is it? The answers are in the box below.

1

2

3

4

5

6

a) It's four thirty.
b) It's twelve thirty.
c) It's six thirty.
d) It's three thirty.
e) It's seven thirty.
f) It's nine thirty.

1	**2**	**3**	**4**	**5**	**6**

Focus Three

He/she/it can/can't ______

Find the missing word. Is it *can* or *can't*?

1 He ______ swim. 2 He ______ talk. 3 It ______ fly. 4 He ______ swim.

5 They ______ talk. 6 He ______ fly. 7 It ______ see. 8 But he ______ see.

1	2	3	4	5	6	7	8

Focus Four

What's wrong with him/her/it?

Find the right answer to each question. The answers are in the box below.

1 What's wrong with her? 2 What's wrong with him? 3 What's wrong with her? 4 What's wrong with him?

a) She's hungry.
b) She's ill.
c) He can't remember his name.
d) Nothing! There's nothing wrong with him.

1	2	3	4

Unit 2 Review

1 Read about episode 2. Find the missing words.

The man is at a police 1__________ . Who 2__________ he? He doesn't 3__________ . He 4__________ got any identification and he 5__________ remember his name. Inspector Marvin is asking, 'What's 6__________ name? 7__________ do you come from?'

The man is 8__________ a clinic now. Dr Roberts is asking him some 9__________ . 'What's two 10__________ two?' 'Look at my eyes. What 11__________ are they?' The man can answer these questions, but he can't 12__________ his name. Inspector Marvin is looking at a 13__________ with some words on it. The words are: 'To Sabina, with 14__________ , Basil.'

know hasn't can't your questions is station where at and remember pen love colour

2 Here is a day at Dr Roberts' clinic. Look at the diary and answer these questions.

DIARY
Dr Roberts

9.30	Mr White
10.30	Mrs Macdonald
11.30	
12.30	Lunch
1.30	Miss Mann
2.30	Mr Jones
3.30	
4.30	Ms Sharp

1 Is Dr Roberts busy at nine thirty?
2 Who is coming at one thirty?
3 What time is Mrs Macdonald's appointment?
4 What time is Dr Roberts free in the morning?
5 What time is Dr Roberts free in the afternoon?
6 What is she doing at twelve thirty?

3 Look at these words. Where do they belong?

✓pen seventeen Thursday ticket yellow black telephone twenty-five Sunday thirty green Wednesday matches eleven Friday

1 numbers	2 colours	3 days of the week	4 things
			pen

Unit 3

WHO IS SABINA?

Preview

1 Can you remember?

1 Where are they?
2 Who is the woman?
3 What is she doing?
4 Can you remember any of her questions?
5 What is the name of the policeman?
6 Do you know the name of the other man?

2 People say these things (1–8) in episode 3. Find good answers (a–h).

1 It's a long flight to London, isn't it?	**a)** I'm not sure. Perhaps in his pocket.
2 What does she look like?	**b)** I'm a doctor. What about you?
3 What do you do?	**c)** At the Palace Hotel.
4 Where are you staying in London?	**d)** To the Palace Hotel.
5 Can we give you a lift?	**e)** Thank you. That's very kind of you.
6 Where do you think it is?	**f)** Yes, about twelve hours.
7 This is my friend.	**g)** She's tall and she has brown eyes.
8 Where are we going now?	**h)** Oh, hello. How do you do?

3 Here are some important words (1–8) from episode 3. Can you find the opposite words (a–h)?

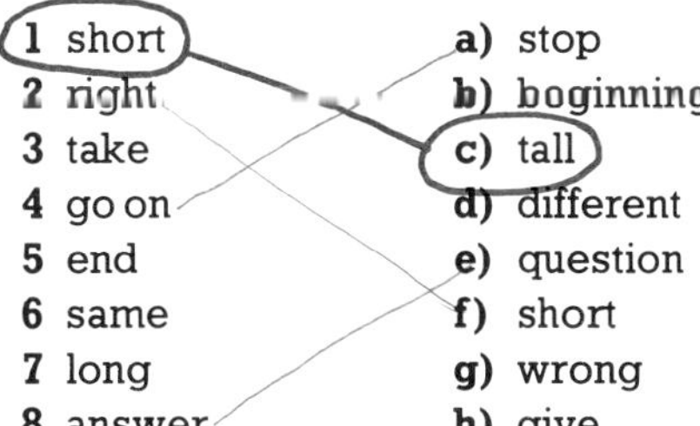

1 short	**a)** stop
2 right	**b)** beginning
3 take	**c)** tall
4 go on	**d)** different
5 end	**e)** question
6 same	**f)** short
7 long	**g)** wrong
8 answer	**h)** give

4 Can you understand these sentences from episode 3?

Think! Try to remember.

Please be careful with it! Don't break it!
It's very important!

Bottle? What's he talking about?

This man isn't a scientist.
A smuggler, perhaps.

THE LOST SECRET

25:04
37:31

Watch episode 3. Don't try to understand every word.

Exercise 1

Look at the pictures (1–6). Find what they are saying (a–f) in each picture.

a) Bring him here!
b) Harry! Stop that!
c) What's in this bottle, sir?
d) Think! Try to remember.
e) I'm pleased to meet you.
f) Where are you from, Sabina?

1	2	3	4	5	6

Exercise 2

Which sentences are true (T)? Which are false (F)?

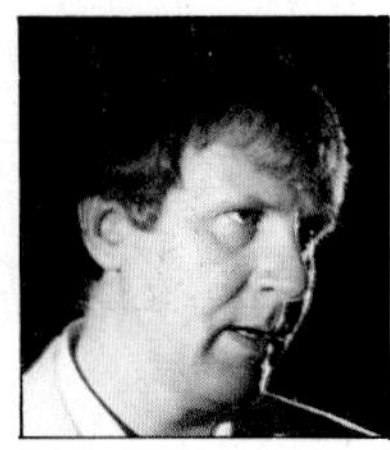

1 This man can remember his name now.
2 He can remember a woman's name.
3 He says he comes from South America and speaks very good English.

4 She comes from South America and speaks very good English.
5 She lives in Argentina but comes from Mexico.
6 She works in a bookshop.

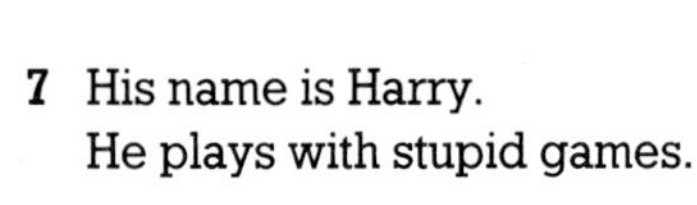

7 His name is Harry.
He plays with stupid games.

8 This man hasn't got a name.

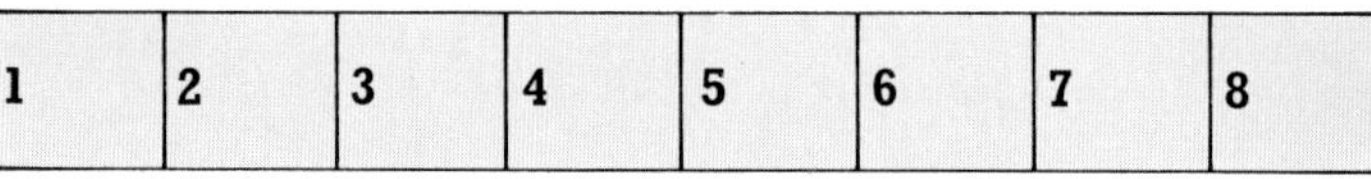

1	2	3	4	5	6	7	8

25:25
29:40

Now watch this part again.

Exercise 3

Find the missing words.

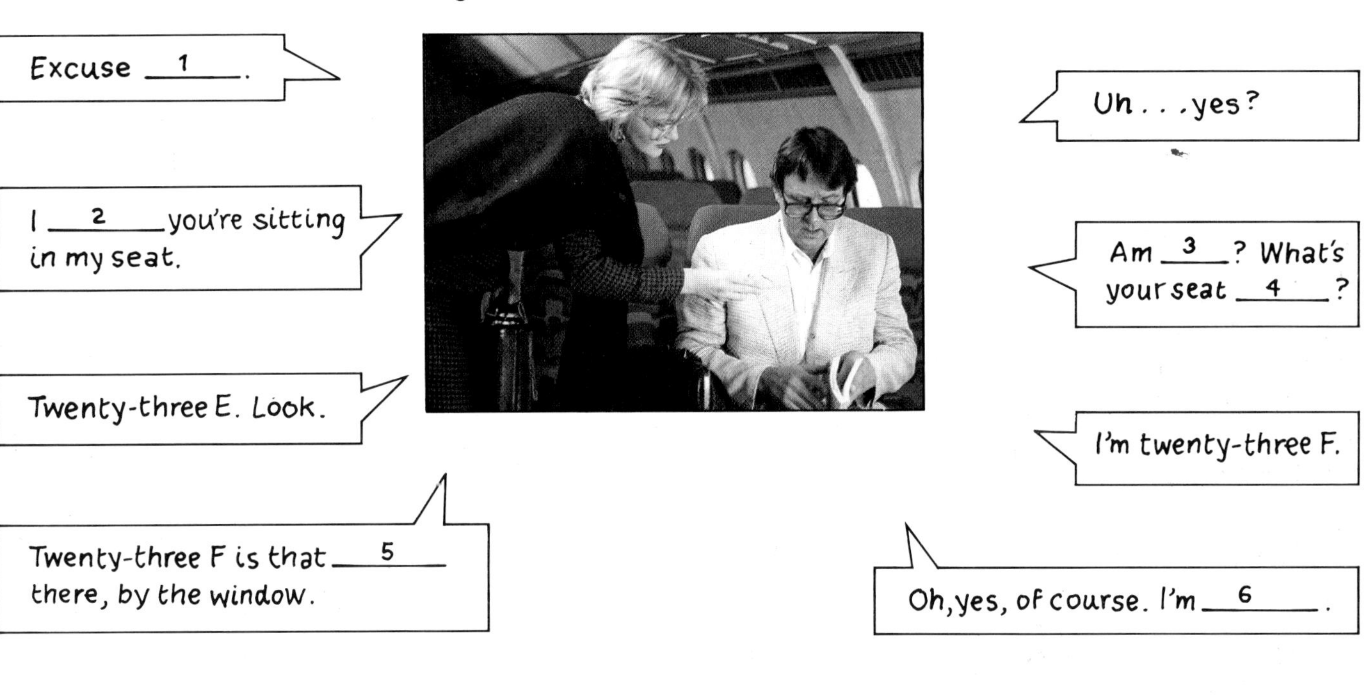

a) I **b**) sorry **c**) me **d**) one **e**) think **f**) number

1	2	3	4	5	6

Exercise 4

Find the words for the numbers on the boarding cards.

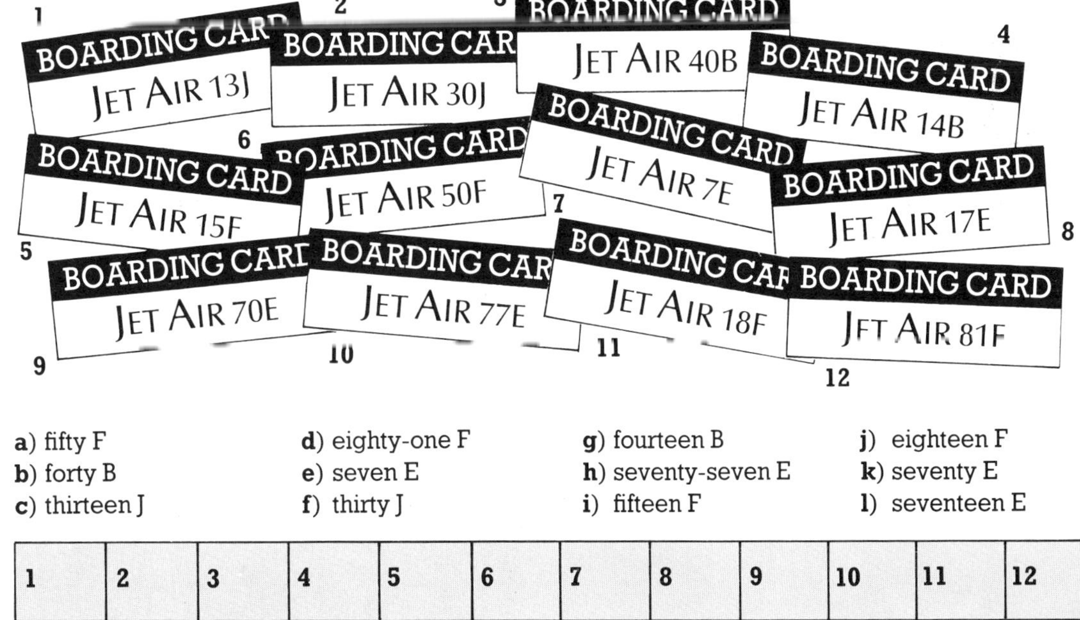

a) fifty F
b) forty B
c) thirteen J
d) eighty-one F
e) seven E
f) thirty J
g) fourteen B
h) seventy-seven E
i) fifteen F
j) eighteen F
k) seventy E
l) seventeen E

1	2	3	4	5	6	7	8	9	10	11	12

Exercise 5

Look at the cartoon strip. Where do the sentences go?

a) What does she look like?
b) What colour is it?
c) Yes. Yes, I am.
d) Don't touch that!
e) That's a nice name.
f) Describe her hair.
g) Here you are.
h) Pardon? I don't understand your question.

1	2	3	4	5	6	7	8

Exercise 6

Look at the questions. Find the right answers.

1 What does Sabina do?
2 Where does she come from?
3 What does her father do?
4 What does her mother do?
5 What do they teach?
6 Why is her English so good?

a) She's a teacher, too.
b) Because both her parents are teachers.
c) She works in a bookshop.
d) History and English.
e) He's a teacher.
f) Argentina.

1	2	3	4	5	6

Exercise 7

Study these words (1–4). Find the right definition (a–d) for each word.

1 teach
2 work
3 history
4 university

a) do a job, usually for money
b) a place where students study, usually after they are 18
c) help someone to learn
d) study of the past

1	2	3	4

30:06
37:31

Now watch this part again.

Exercise 8

Where do these sentences go?

a) In a hotel.
b) Oh, I don't know. By bus?
c) We're landing now.
d) Oh, thank you. That's very kind of you.
e) Don't worry.
f) Go on with your story.

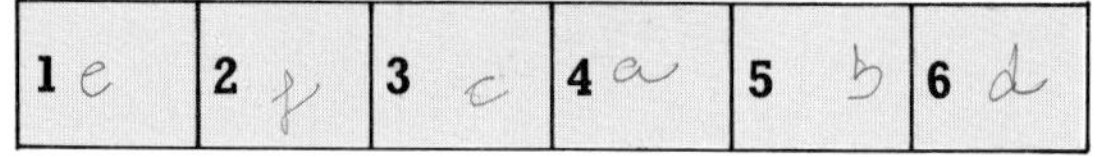

Exercise 9

Find a sentence that means almost the same thing.

1 That's very kind of you.
2 Don't worry.
3 Go on with your story.
4 Can we give you a lift?

a) Would you like to come in our car?
b) Thank you very much.
c) It's all right. It isn't a problem.
d) Tell me more.

1	2	3	4

Exercise 10

What are the missing words?

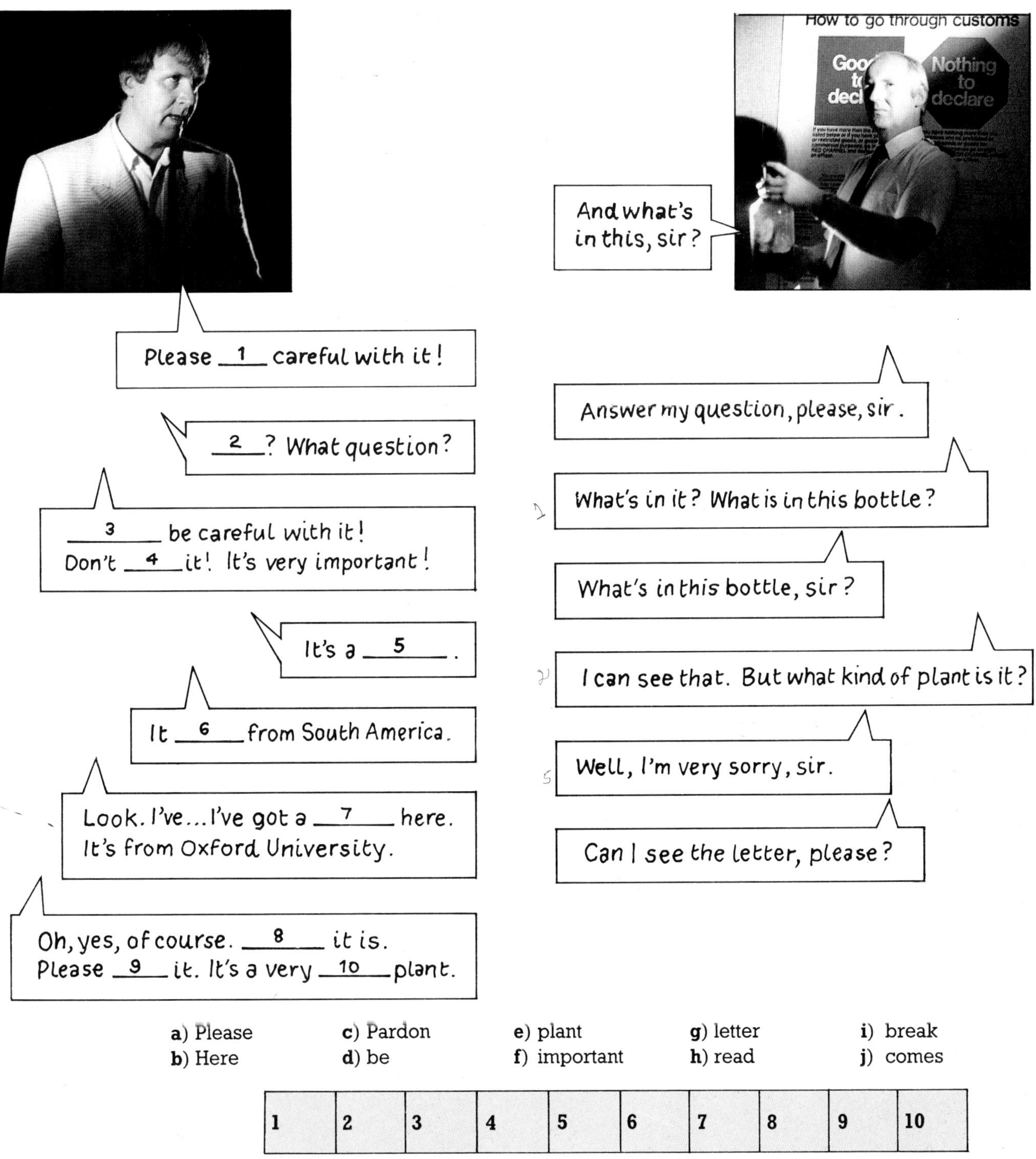

a) Please
b) Here
c) Pardon
d) be
e) plant
f) important
g) letter
h) read
i) break
j) comes

1	2	3	4	5	6	7	8	9	10

Exercise 11

True (T) or false (F)?

1 The customs officer is answering questions about the plant.
2 The man is answering questions about the plant.
3 The plant is from Oxford University.
4 It comes from South America.
5 The man has got a letter from a university about the plant.
6 The customs officer can't read the letter.

1	2	3	4	5	6

Now read the story.

In Dr Roberts' clinic

"What was in the bottle?" Dr Roberts asks the man. Inspector Marvin is listening. He is very interested.

"Bottle? What's he talking about?" he asks her.

"There was a plant in it," the man answers.

"A plant? What kind of plant?" she asks. She wants to know more too.

The man tries to answer the question. But he can't. "It . . . it was in the bottle," he says.

Dr Roberts looks at Inspector Marvin and then asks the man the same question again. "What kind of plant was it?"

The man tries to remember. But he can't. "It . . . it was from South America," he tells her.

Dr Roberts looks at him. She can see that he can't answer any more questions. She goes over to Inspector Marvin. "A plant from South America. Perhaps he's a scientist. A botanist, perhaps," she says.

But Inspector Marvin doesn't think so. "This man isn't a scientist. A smuggler, perhaps!" he tells her. They both look at the man in the chair by the window.

"A smuggler? But he can't be. Look at him!" she says.

The man isn't listening to them. He is thinking about the customs officer at the airport. He can remember more now! He showed the customs officer the letter from Oxford University. The officer read it and told him it was all right. He took the plant with him, and then . . . then . . . there were two men at the airport with Sabina. Yes! He can remember them now!

Exercise 12

Study these words (1–8) from the story. Find the definition (a–h) for each word.

1 science		**a**)	a word we use when we aren't sure; when we don't really know
2 was/were		**b**)	a man or woman who brings drugs, alcohol, etc into a country and doesn't tell the customs officer about them
3 perhaps		**c**)	the study of nature: chemistry, physics, biology, botany etc
4 scientist		**d**)	past form of 'is' and 'are'; we use these words with other words like 'yesterday', 'in 1960', 'last month', etc
5 botanist		**e**)	a man or woman who studies and knows a lot about physics, chemistry, etc
6 smuggler		**f**)	want to know more about something
7 plants		**g**)	trees, flowers and other things that live but are not animals
8 interested		**h**)	a man or woman who studies trees, flowers and other plants

1 c	2 d	3 a	4 e	5 h	6 b	7 G	8 f

Exercise 13

True (T) or false (F)?

1. The man can't answer the question 'What kind of plant was it?' T
2. Dr Roberts isn't interested in the plant. F
3. Inspector Marvin wants to know more about the plant.
4. He doesn't think the man is a smuggler. F
5. Dr Roberts doesn't think the man is a smuggler. T
6. A botanist is a man or woman who smuggles plants into a country.

1	2	3	4	5	6

Exercise 14

Can you remember this too? Can you remember the missing sentences?

a) No? It doesn't matter. I know yours.
b) Sorry, but sometimes Harry can be a little . . . strange.
c) Over there! Put it there!
d) The gum! Don't chew gum!
e) This is my friend, the professor. Do you remember? I told you about him on the plane.
f) That stupid game! Are you a child or a man?
g) Yes, I'm very pleased to meet you too.
h) No! Don't put it in your pocket!

1	2	3	4	5	6	7	8

Focus One

What does he/she do? What is he/she doing?

What's the right answer: **a**) or **b**)?

1 What does she do?
a) She's working in an office.
b) She's a doctor.

2 What is she doing?
a) She's working in her office.
b) She's a doctor.

3 What does he do?
a) He's looking at a plant.
b) He's a customs officer.

4 What is he doing?
a) He's looking at a plant.
b) He's a customs officer.

1	2	3	4

Focus Two

What do you do?

Find the answers to the questions. The answers are in the box below.

a) I'm a bookseller. I sell books.
b) I'm a teacher. I teach history in a university.
c) I'm a doctor. I work in a hospital.
d) I'm a policeman. I work in a police station.

1	2	3	4

Focus Three

What does he/she look like?

Find the right sentence for each picture. The sentences are in the box below.

a) He's handsome.
b) He's of medium height.
c) He's ugly.
d) He's fat.
e) He's short.
f) He's tall.
g) She's beautiful.
h) She's thin.

1	2	3	4	5	6	7	8

Focus Four

Who/What/Where is ______ ?

Find the missing word. Is it *Who*, *What* or *Where?*

1	2	3

Unit 3

Review

1 What is Sabina saying? Find the missing words.

'My name 1____________ Sabina. I 2____________ from Argentina but I 3____________ in Mexico City. My parents 4____________ in Mexico City too. They 5____________ at the university. My father 6____________ history and my mother 7____________ English. I 8____________ in a bookshop. I 9____________ books very much.'

2 Write the verbs in their full forms.

Example: He's a professor. *He is a professor.*

1 I'm sorry.
2 They're here.
3 They don't know.
4 She doesn't think so.
5 He's tall.
6 She's got short hair.
7 What's that man doing?
8 I can't see.
9 I haven't got my luggage.
10 I've got the answer.

3 Look at the words (1–12). Find the meanings (a–l).

1 touch
2 case
3 flight
4 describe
5 medium height
6 beautiful
7 child
8 game
9 everything
10 fine
11 luggage
12 sometimes

a) say how someone or something looks
b) very good-looking
c) put your hand on
d) not tall, not short
e) box, bag, etc for carrying things
f) trip in a plane
g) all things
h) not all but some of the time
i) something you can play with
j) bags, cases, etc
k) young boy or girl
l) good

4 Test. Complete these sentences. Can you answer the questions?

1 What ____________ Sabina do?
2 What ____________ you do?
3 Where ____________ she live?
4 Where ____________ you live?
5 What colour ____________ her hair?
6 What colour ____________ her eyes?
7 What colour ____________ your eyes?
8 What colour ____________ your hair?

Unit 4

FOOTPRINTS IN THE SAND

Preview

1 Can you remember episode 3? Are these sentences true or false?

1. This man and this woman met on a plane.
2. She lives in Mexico but comes from Argentina.
3. She has a plant in her briefcase.
4. Two men were waiting at the airport.
5. The two men knew him but they didn't know her.
6. They got into a car and drove away with the man.
7. A man and a woman followed them.

2 People say these things (1–5) in this episode. Find good answers (a–e).

1. Go on. You checked in, what happened then?
2. Was it warm in Mexico City?
3. This is your book, isn't it?
4. You were in a car with them. Where did you go with them?
5. How would you like to pay?

- **a)** To a hotel.
- **b)** Yes, it was.
- **c)** Yes, it is.
- **d)** By credit card. Would you like to see it?
- **e)** I spoke to the receptionist.

3 Study these words from episode 4.

rain tomorrow foreign
archeology believe plans dinner

Now use the words in these sentences.

1. How many ______ languages do you speak?
2. Today is Tuesday, so ______ is Wednesday.
3. Would you like to have ______ with me tonight?
4. It was fine in the morning, but later it began to ______.
5. That's not true. I can't ______ it.
6. Are you busy next week? What are your ______?
7. ______ is the study of very old civilisations.

4 Here are some more things people say. Who do you think says them?

The small memories are as important as the big ones.

Two years ago I wrote a book.

You are an expert on the Mepatecs, aren't you?

They were a very great civilisation – and then something very strange happened to them.

37:43
50:22

Watch episode 4. Then do exercises 1 and 2.

Exercise 1

What are they saying in the pictures?

a) What are you watching?
b) Perhaps we can all have dinner together?
c) I can carry it. It's all right!
d) This form came from Inspector Marvin. Can you sign it, please?
e) They're on a beach. There are waves.

1	2	3	4	5

Exercise 2

True (T) or false (F)?

1 He still can't remember his name.
2 He remembers a book about a lost civilisation.
3 This man's name isn't 'Sign' but it's a name like 'Sign'.
4 He wrote a book about a great civilisation in South America.

1	2	3	4

38.03
41.04

Now watch this part again. Then do exercises 3 to 6.

Exercise 3

Where do the words and sentences go?

a) Go on.
b) He said he was a professor.
c) Sign? Go on. Think of a name like 'sign'.
d) It doesn't matter.
e) The man with Sabina.
f) He told me his name, but I can't remember it.

1	2	3	4	5	6

Exercise 4

Find the right definitions (a–d) for the words and phrases (1–4).

1 She introduced him to me.
2 foreign
3 form
4 Can you sign it, please?

a) a document, paper, etc
b) She said, 'This is ______ (name).'
c) Please write your name on it.
d) from another country

1	2	3	4

Exercise 5

Find the missing sentences.

Yes, I've got another name for you, a professor. He met him at the airport. He was with Sabina at the airport. His name's Professor Sline. 6

a) Do you know him?
b) He says he can't remember!
c) Well, what have you got?
d) Please take a seat.
e) Do you know any more about him?
f) This one's very interesting, sir.
g) How do you spell that?
h) It's all very strange.
i) Ah! Hello, Dr Roberts.

1	2	3	4	5	6	7	8	9

Exercise 6

What did they say: **a**) or **b**)?

Do you still ___1___ he's a smuggler?
a) think b) thinking

I ___2___ know.
a) don't b) doesn't

Look, sir. I've ___3___ something here.
a) get b) got

Is it the man we're ___4___?
a) look for b) looking for

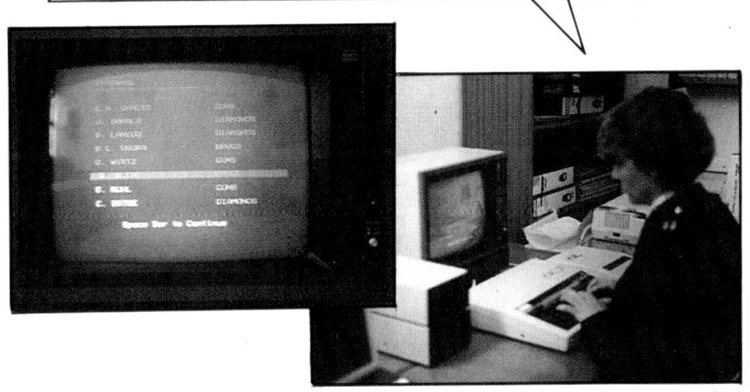

1	2	3	4

41.05
44.05

Now watch this part again. Then do exercises 7, 8 and 9.

Exercise 7

What's wrong with the story? There is something in the story that isn't right. Can you find it?

The Lost Secret

Dr Roberts is at the clinic again. The man is sitting in front of the television.

"Hello. How are you?" she asks.

"I'm fine," the man answers. But he doesn't look at her. The doctor looks at the television. She can see pictures but she can't hear anything.

"What's wrong with the television?" she asks.

"Nothing, there's nothing wrong with it," the man answers. He still doesn't look at her. "I don't want to listen to it. I only want to watch it," he says.

"I see. What are you watching?" she asks.

The man isn't really listening to her. He is very interested in the pictures on the television. It is a film. A young man and a woman are on a beach. There are waves and there is water.

"Are you all right?" the doctor asks.

"Look, look, the rain! Footprints! Footprints in the water!" the man says.

The doctor doesn't understand.

"What are you saying?" she asks.

"The rain! It's washing away the footprints! And the footprints are my memories. The rain washes memories away like footprints in the water!" he tells her.

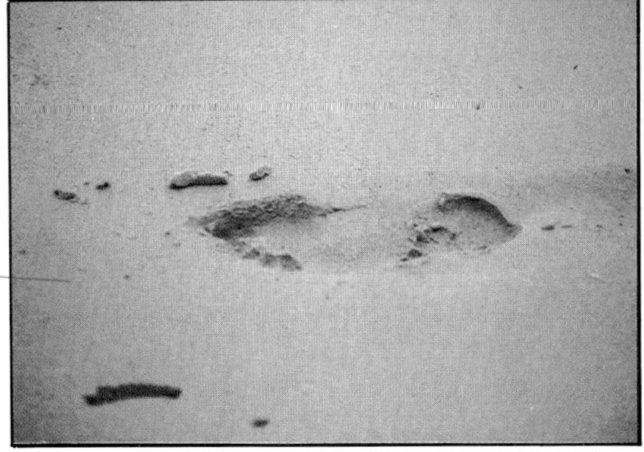

Exercise 8

Find the right sentence (a–d) for each picture (1–4).

1

2

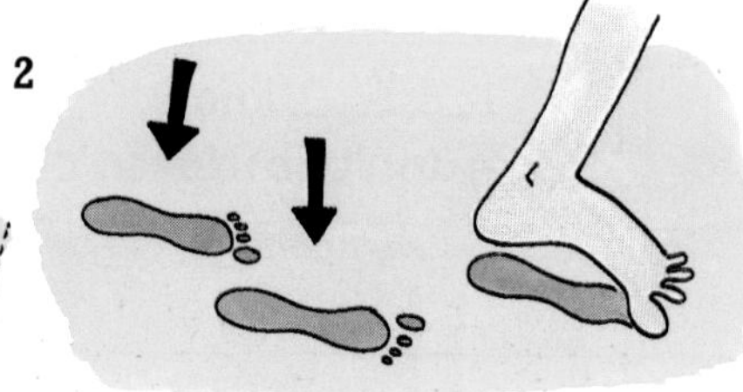

3

4

a) The weather's bad. It's raining.
b) The rain is washing the footprints away.
c) Look at the footprints in the sand.
d) He's washing his face.

1	2	3	4

Now let's go on with the story! The man remembers a lot more now. He remembers that the professor and Sabina gave him a lift in their car and that they drove into London. They talked about the weather. The professor asked a lot of questions.

Exercise 9

Read the professor's questions. What is the right answer: **a)** or **b)**?

1 Was it warm in Mexico City?
a) Yes, it is. It's very warm.
b) Yes, it was. It was very warm.

2 Yes, Mexico City is always much warmer than London, isn't it? And did it rain?
a) Yes, it does. It rains a lot.
b) Yes, it did. It rained a lot.

3 Oh yes, I remember the rain in Mexico. 'The rain washes memories away like footprints in the sand.'
a) What do you say?
b) What did you say?

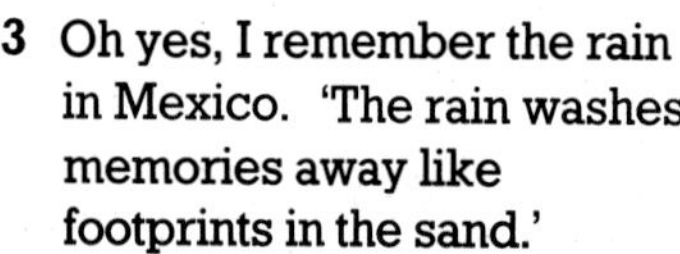

4 You are an expert on the Mepatecs, aren't you?
a) Yes – yes, I am.
b) Yes – yes, you are.

5 And this is your book, isn't it?
a) Yes – yes, that is my book.
b) Yes – yes, this is my book.

6 Don't you remember what the Mepatecs said? They said, 'We can wash memories away like footprints in the sand'.
a) Yes. You know a lot about the Mepatecs.
b) Yes. I know a lot about the Mepatecs.

Not as much as you. You wrote this book, didn't you? And you are Dr Ross Orwell, aren't you?

1	2	3	4	5	6

44.06
50.22

Now watch this part again. Then do exercises 10 to 14.

Exercise 10

Read the story. There are three things wrong with this part of the story. Can you find them?

The Lost Secret

The man can remember something very, very important now. "He said my name. Dr Ross Orwell!"

Dr Roberts looks at him.

"Doctor Ross Orwell?"

"Yes! I'm an archeologist!"

"And Sline had a copy of your book."

"Yes. Two years ago I wrote a book about the Mepatecs. They were a great civilisation in South America," he tells her.

He stands up and goes into the other room.

"Dr Orwell? What are you doing?" Dr Roberts asks.

But Orwell doesn't answer. There are a lot of books in the other room. Orwell takes a very big one and opens it.

"J . . . K . . . L . . . M. Here we are!" he says.

"What are you looking for?" Dr Roberts asks.

"The Mepatecs. They were a very great civilisation – and then something very strange happened to them," Orwell says.

"Don't talk about the Mepatecs now, Dr Orwell."

"But don't you understand? There was a very important secret," says Orwell. But Dr Roberts doesn't want to hear about the Mepatecs now.

"We can talk about the Mepatecs later. Tell me about Professor Sline and Sabina. Where did they take you?" she asks.

The Lost Secret

Orwell doesn't want to answer the question. "Where did they take me? That isn't important," he tells her. He wants to talk about the Mepatecs.

Dr Roberts stops him.

"You were in a car with them. Where did you go with them?" she asks him again.

"To a hotel," Orwell answers. He is still looking at the big book.

"What did you do there?"

"I checked in."

"Go on. You checked in. What happened then?"

"I spoke to the receptionist. But that isn't important," Orwell says again.

He can't understand why she is asking him these questions.

"Please believe me. I'm trying to help you. Try to remember everything. Everything! The small memories aren't as important as the big memories. Now tell me more about the hotel," Dr Roberts says.

Orwell still doesn't think her question is important. But he tries to answer it.

"It was a small hotel . . . near Oxford Street, I think."

"And what was the name of the hotel?" Dr Roberts asks him.

Orwell thinks. But he can't remember the name.

Exercise 11

Here are some of the things the receptionist said to Orwell (1–6). Put Orwell's answers (a–f) in the right order.

1 Good evening, sir.

2 Ah, yes. Dr Orwell. Would you fill in this form, please?

3 Yes, Dr Orwell. Would you like a newspaper in the morning?

4 OK, sir. And how long are you staying?

5 Well, let's say three, and if you want to leave before, just let us know. And how would you like to pay?

6 Yes, please. And here is your key, sir.

a) Yes, *The Times*.

b) Thank you.

c) Good evening. My name is Orwell. I've got a reservation. A single room, with a shower.

d) Yes, of course . . . . Is that all right?

e) By credit card. Would you like to see it?

f) I'm not sure. Three days, perhaps two.

1	2	3	4	5	6

Exercise 12

What does it mean: **a**) or **b**)?

1 I've got a reservation.
a) There is something wrong with me.
b) You've got a room for me in my name.

2 a single room
a) a room for one person
b) a room for two people

1	2

Exercise 13

True (T) or false (F)?

1 The receptionist also says, 'I think I'm catching a cold.'
2 'I'm catching a cold' means 'It's very cold here.'
3 Orwell says, 'I'm catching a cold too.'
4 The receptionist thinks Orwell could give her something for her cold, but he can't.
5 You can also say in English, 'I've got a cold.'
6 This means 'I'm ill. There's something wrong with my nose or throat.'

1	2	3	4	5	6

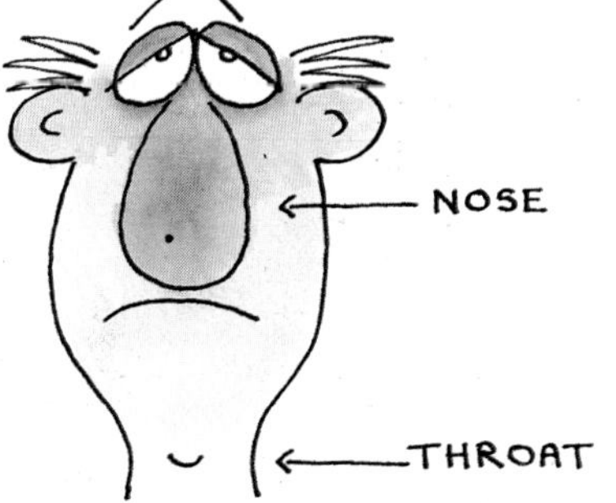

Has he got a cold?

Exercise 14

Find the missing words.

a) tomorrow **c**) meeting **e**) his **g**) case **i**) lift **k**) room **m**) busy **o**) kind
b) meet **d**) your **f**) dinner **h**) drink **j**) carry **l**) car **n**) like **p**) sorry

1	2	3	4	5	6	7	8

9	10	11	12	13	14	15	16

Focus One

is/are or *was/were*?

Is the right word **a**) or **b**)?

1 She ______ busy.
a) is **b**) was

2 He ______ happy.
a) is **b**) was

3 His hair ______ long.
a) is **b**) was

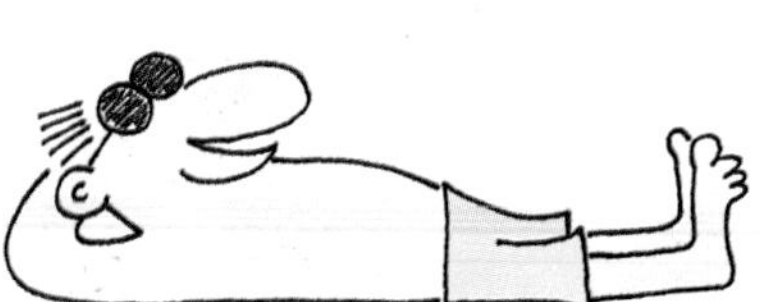

4 It ______ warm.
a) is **b**) was

5 They ______ on the plane.
a) are **b**) were

6 She ______ a child.
a) is **b**) was

1	2	3	4	5	6

Focus Two

What do they want to do?

Find the right sentence for each picture.

1

2

3
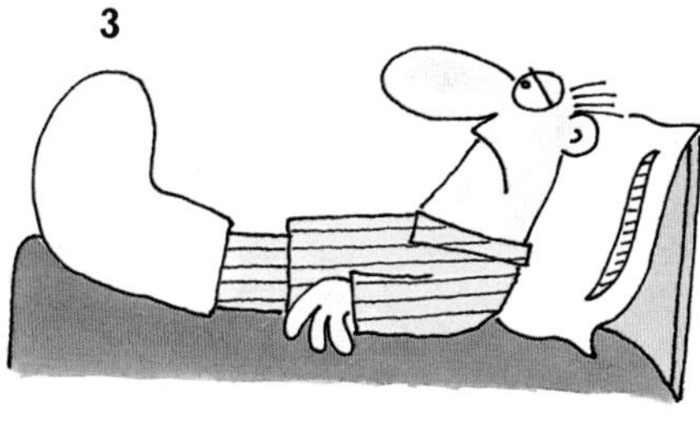

4

5

6

a) He wants to fly.
b) I want to have a drink.
c) She wants to watch television.
d) He wants to walk.
e) I want to listen to the radio.
f) She wants to read a book.

1	2	3	4	5	6

Focus Three

What did he do at ______ o'clock?

Find the right sentence for each picture.

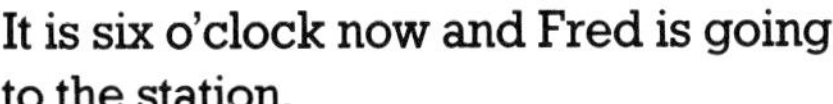

It is six o'clock now and Fred is going to the station.

1 At five o'clock ______ .

2 At four o'clock ______ .

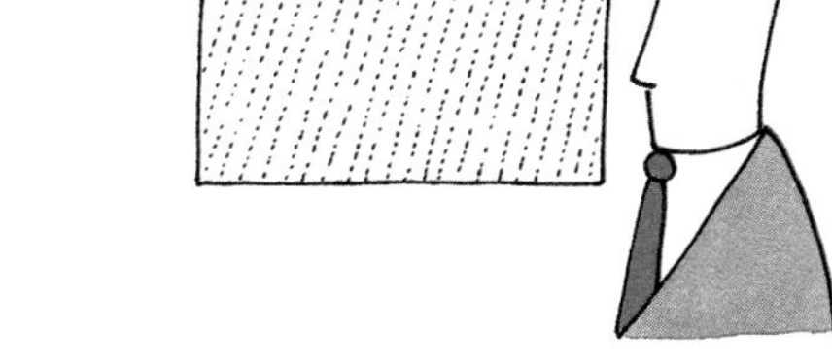

3 At three o'clock ______ .

4 At two o'clock ______ .

5 At one o'clock ______ .

a) he talked to his boss
b) he wrote a letter
c) he phoned his friend
d) he watched television
e) it rained

1	2	3	4	5

Focus Four

today/tomorrow/yesterday

August						
Sunday	Monday	Tuesday	Wednesday	Thursday	Friday	Saturday
				1	2	3
4	5	6	7 (today)	8	9	10
11	12	13	14	15	16	17
18	19	20	21	22	23	24
25	26	27	28	29	30	31

Let's say that today is Wednesday, 7 August. That is today's date. What day was it yesterday? And what about tomorrow? What day is it tomorrow?

Find the right word: **a**) or **b**)?

1 Yesterday ______ Tuesday, 6 August.
a) is
b) was

2 Tomorrow ______ Thursday, 8 August.
a) is
b) was

1	2

Unit 4

Review

1 Tell the story in the past tense. Can you remember the man's name?

The man (is) 1 was in the garden with Dr Roberts. Her secretary (speaks) 2__________ to her. She (has) 3__________ a form in her hand. She (says) 4__________ the word 'sign'. Suddenly the man (remembers) 5__________ something. The professor's name (is) 6__________ like 'sign'!

Then he (remembers) 7__________ something more. He (is) 8__________ in a car with the professor. There (is) 9__________ a book in the professor's hand. The professor (asks) 10__________ a question about the book. Then he (says) 11__________ a name – 12__________ !

2 What do you think happens in episode 5? Look at this picture and answer the questions.

1. Where are they?
   - In an office?
   - At a police station?
   - On an aeroplane?
   - In a restaurant?
2. What are they doing?
3. Who is coming in a few minutes?
4. Why is the man there?
   - Because he wants to see Sabina.
   - Because he is hungry and likes the food here.
   - Because something strange happened after Sline left the hotel.
   - Because he wants some information about the Mepatecs.

3 Test. Complete these sentences. Can you answer the questions too?

1. What __________ you do yesterday?
2. Did you __________ television last night?
3. __________ you do that every day?
4. Where __________ you born?
5. __________ do you spell your name?
6. What __________ you like to do this evening?
7. What __________ the weather like in your country?
8. What __________ the weather like yesterday?
9. __________ it rain last week?
10. __________ it often rain in your country?
11. Is the weather there usually warmer __________ it is in England?
12. Is it as cold __________ it is here?
13. What do you know __________ the Mepatecs?
14. I'm sorry, but I'm not very interested __________ your questions.
15. Don't worry. It __________ matter.

Unit 5

ONE O'CLOCK AT ALFREDO'S

Preview

1 Can you remember episode 4?

1 He can remember something very important now. What is it?
2 What does he do?
3 Who were the Mepatecs?
4 Where did he go with the professor and Sabina?
5 Who said, 'The rain washes memories away like footprints in the sand'? What do you think this means?

2 These questions (1–6) are from episode 5. Find good answers (a–f).

1 How do I get to Alfredo's restaurant?
2 Where is he? Why isn't he here now?
3 Would you like something to drink?
4 Why are you helping him?
5 Are you ill?
6 Are you drunk?

a) He's late, but don't worry.
b) Yes, I am. Can you get me a doctor?
c) Of course I'm not! I'm drinking orange juice, not whisky!
d) Go out of the hotel and turn left. Then walk two streets and turn right.
e) Yes, some orange juice, please.
f) Because he's a friend. A good friend.

3 Here are some important words (1–8) from episode 5. Can you find the opposite words (a–h)?

1 early
2 left
3 always
4 heavy
5 destroy
6 easy
7 a little
8 sleep

a) right
b) a lot
c) late
d) difficult
e) wake up
f) light
g) never
h) make

4 Here are some more things people say. Who do you think says them? Is it Sabina, Professor Sline, Dr Roberts or Dr Orwell?

Don't tell the police! Or you'll never see the manuscript or the plant again!

You said you met Sabina at the restaurant, but she was alone. What happened then?

He'll be here soon. I told you. Please, sit down.

Do your friends usually steal things?

50:35
63:05

Watch episode 5. Then do exercises 1, 2 and 3.

Exercise 1

Match the pictures (1–4) with the sentences (a–d).

a) He wasn't hungry but she ordered some lasagne for him.
b) When he got there, she was alone.
c) It was early in the morning. He woke him up.
d) She asked about it. They had it there and she bought it.

1	2	3	4

Exercise 2

Who said this? And in which picture?

1 What do you want? Why are you doing this?
2 Are you ready to order, or would you like some more time?
3 Thank you. I'll take it.
4 Why don't you sit down?

1	2	3	4

Exercise 3

Can you answer these questions now?

1 Why was the professor late?
2 Where did Orwell think his manuscript was when the professor phoned him?
3 What did Sabina order?
4 What was the book about?

50:56
53:49

Watch this part of the episode again. Then do exercises 4 and 5.

Exercise 4

Find the missing words.

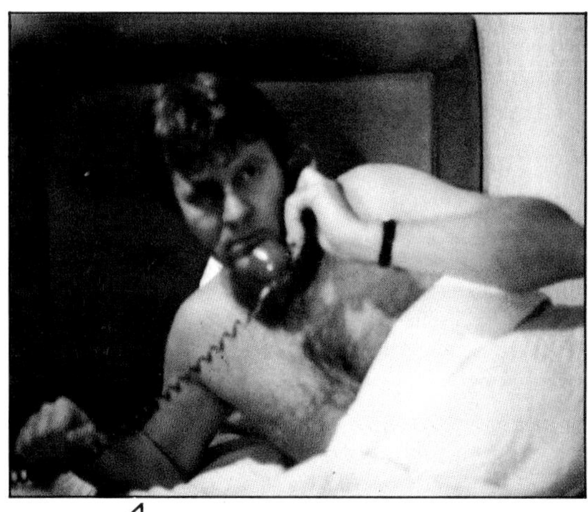

I know it's rather ___1___, Dr Orwell. I'm very sorry, but it's ___2___. It's about your ___3___.

Do you know what time this is?

My what? I don't think I ___4___.

Come, come, Dr Orwell, your manuscript! I'm ___5___ you know what I'm talking about. It's in ___6___ of me, and it's very interesting.

What do you ___7___? That isn't possible! I've got my briefcase, it's here, ___8___ to my bed.

I know it, but ___9___ it, Dr Orwell. Look ___10___ it. Can you see your manuscript?

a) early
b) front
c) important
d) inside
e) manuscript
f) mean
g) next
h) open
i) sure
j) understand

1	2	3	4	5	6	7	8	9	10

Exercise 5

What else happened? Which sentences are true (T) and which are false (F)?

1 Sline phoned Orwell at his hotel.
2 It was eight thirty (8.30) in the morning.
3 When Orwell looked inside his briefcase he saw his manuscript.
4 Sline wanted to see Orwell again.
5 He gave Orwell the name of an Italian restaurant.
6 He gave Orwell the address of the restaurant too.

1	2	3	4	5	6

53:50
54:30

Do you remember what happened when Orwell spoke to the receptionist? Watch again if you can't remember, then do exercises 6, 7 and 8.

Exercise 6

Here are four questions you can ask when you want to go somewhere and don't know where it is. But which question did Orwell ask when he spoke to the receptionist?

1 Excuse me. Where is *Alfredo's*?
2 How do I get to *Alfredo's restaurant*? It's in *Martin Street*.
3 Can you tell me the way to *Alfredo's restaurant* in *Martin Street*?
4 Can you tell me how to get to *Alfredo's restaurant* in *Martin Street*?

Exercise 7

And what did the woman tell him: **a**), **b**) or **c**)?

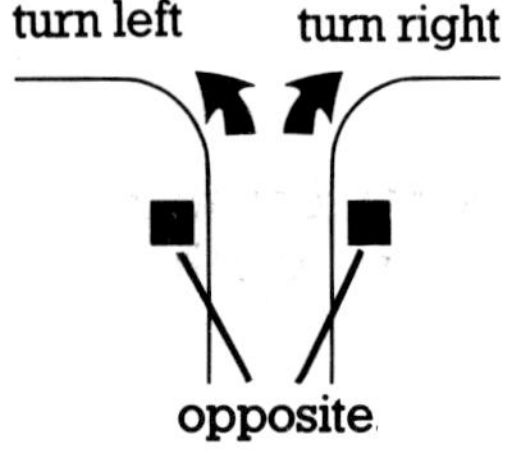

a) Go out of the hotel and turn right. Then take the first right and then turn right again. Then there's a cinema on your left. Turn left again and Alfredo's is just opposite.
b) Go out of the hotel and turn left. Then take the second left and the first right. Turn right again and Alfredo's is just opposite.
c) Go out of the hotel and turn left. Then take the first right and the second left. Then there's a cinema on your left. Turn left again and Alfredo's is just opposite.

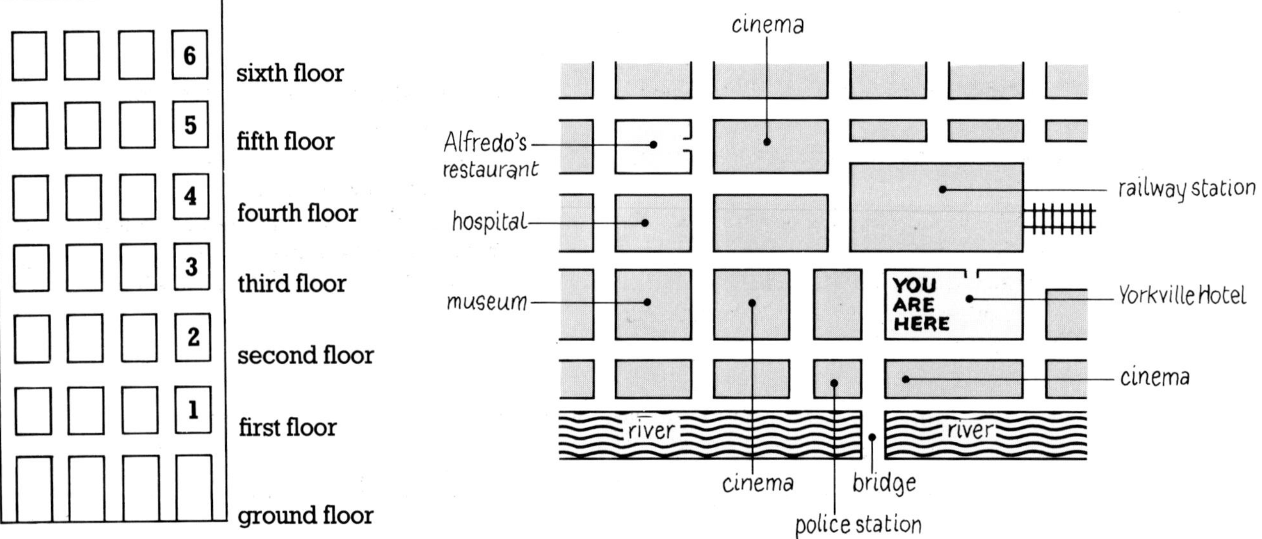

Exercise 8

Look at the two wrong answers from exercise 7 again. Where are you if you choose the two wrong answers?

55:27
56:07

Now watch this part of the episode again. Dr Roberts goes to the bookshop.

Exercise 9

This is what the woman in the shop said. Find Dr Roberts' answers (a–f).

1 Can I help you, madam?
2 The Mepatecs? What's the title?
3 Who wrote it?
4 Yes, we have.
5 It's here.
6 Twelve pounds fifty (£12.50).

a) Good.
b) Thank you. I'll take it.
c) Yes, I'm looking for a book about the Mepatecs.
d) How much is it?
e) Dr Ross Orwell. Have you got it?
f) It's called *The Mepatecs – The Lost Civilisation.* It's an archeology book.

1	2	3	4	5	6

56:09
57:53

Exercise 10

In the car Dr Orwell and Dr Roberts talked about the Mepatecs. Do you remember what they said? Watch this part again and then say which sentences are true (T) and which are false (F).

1 Dr Roberts doesn't know anything about the Mepatecs.
2 She knows something about them, but only a little.
3 The Mepatec civilisation suddenly came to an end.
4 This happened a long time ago.
5 Orwell thinks this happened because they used a drug.
6 He says other people controlled the Mepatecs with a drug.
7 The Mepatecs made a drug.
8 It destroyed the memory.
9 He says it destroyed the Mepatecs too.
10 He says nobody knows why their civilisation suddenly disappeared.

1	2	3	4	5	6	7	8	9	10

Exercise 11

How do we say these numbers?

150 55 75 86 99 250 2000 3000 2500

Exercise 12

What happened when Orwell went to the restaurant? Read this story and then answer the questions with yes (Y) or no (N).

The Lost Secret

The woman in reception said that the restaurant was easy to find. But it wasn't easy. It was difficult to find. It was exactly one o'clock when Orwell got there. Sabina was at the table, waiting. She was alone. She smiled at Orwell. But he didn't smile at her.

"Why don't you sit down?" she said.

"Where is he? Why isn't he here now? He said one o'clock," Orwell said.

"He'll be here soon. I told you. Please sit down," Sabina said, and smiled again.

The waiter brought the menus.

"Would you like something to drink?" he asked.

Sabina ordered a glass of orange juice.

"It is fresh, isn't it?"

"Of course, madam. Everything in our restaurant is fresh," the waiter told her.

Orwell ordered an orange juice too. Sabina told him that the food was very good. But he wasn't hungry.

"Why don't you have some lasagne?" Sabina asked.

"I don't want anything!" he said loudly. He was angry. He wanted to see the professor. He didn't want to eat or talk about food. The waiter came back. Sabina smiled at him.

1 Was the restaurant easy to find?
2 Was the professor in the restaurant when Orwell got there?
3 Was Sabina there?
4 Did Sabina order something to drink?
5 Did she order wine?
6 Did Orwell want anything to eat?
7 Look at the photograph. Is Sabina smiling?
8 Can you see Orwell's face in the photograph?
9 Do you think he is smiling too?

1	2	3	4	5	6	7	8	9

Exercise 13

Who is smiling here?
The man on the left? Or the man on the right?

Which woman is smiling here?

59:31
60:30

Watch this part of the episode again, and then do exercises 14 and 15.

Exercise 14

Can you find the ten missing words (a–j)?

a) like
b) so
c) speak
d) think
e) all
f) doesn't
g) isn't
h) hungry
i) slept
j) sleep

1	2	3	4	5	6	7	8	9	10

Exercise 15

What do you think 'some' means in these sentences?

1 But I'll have some.
a) a lot
b) a little

2 Would you like some wine?
a) only one glass
b) a glass, or perhaps a bottle

1	2

60:30
63:05

And what happened after that? You can watch the rest of the episode now, and then do exercises 16, 17 and 18.

Exercise 16

Find the word or phrase closest in meaning: **a**), **b**) or **c**)?

1 a friend
a) someone you don't know
b) someone you know
c) someone you know and like

2 steal
a) take something that is not yours
b) give something to someone
c) buy

3 heavy traffic
a) cars and other things
b) a lot of cars, buses, etc
c) very bad weather and rain

4 my friends never steal things
a) they don't steal anything
b) they steal some things
c) they steal things all the time

5 Do your friends usually steal things?
a) Do they want to steal things?
b) Do they like to steal things?
c) Do they steal things again and again?

1	2	3	4	5

Exercise 17

True (T) or false (F)?

1 When Sline came into the restaurant he ordered some tomato juice.
2 He likes tomato juice.
3 He would like some tomato juice.
4 Orwell isn't well because he drank a lot of wine and whisky in the hotel. He is drunk.
5 Orwell isn't well because there was something in his orange juice.

1	2	3	4	5

Exercise 18

What happened then? Answer yes (Y) or no (N).

1 Did the waiter come?
2 Did Sline and Sabina eat some food?
3 Did they leave the restaurant with Orwell?
4 Did they pay the waiter for the food?

1	2	3	4

Focus One

How long ago was it?

Today is Saturday. What happened to Orwell this week? Fill in the missing words.

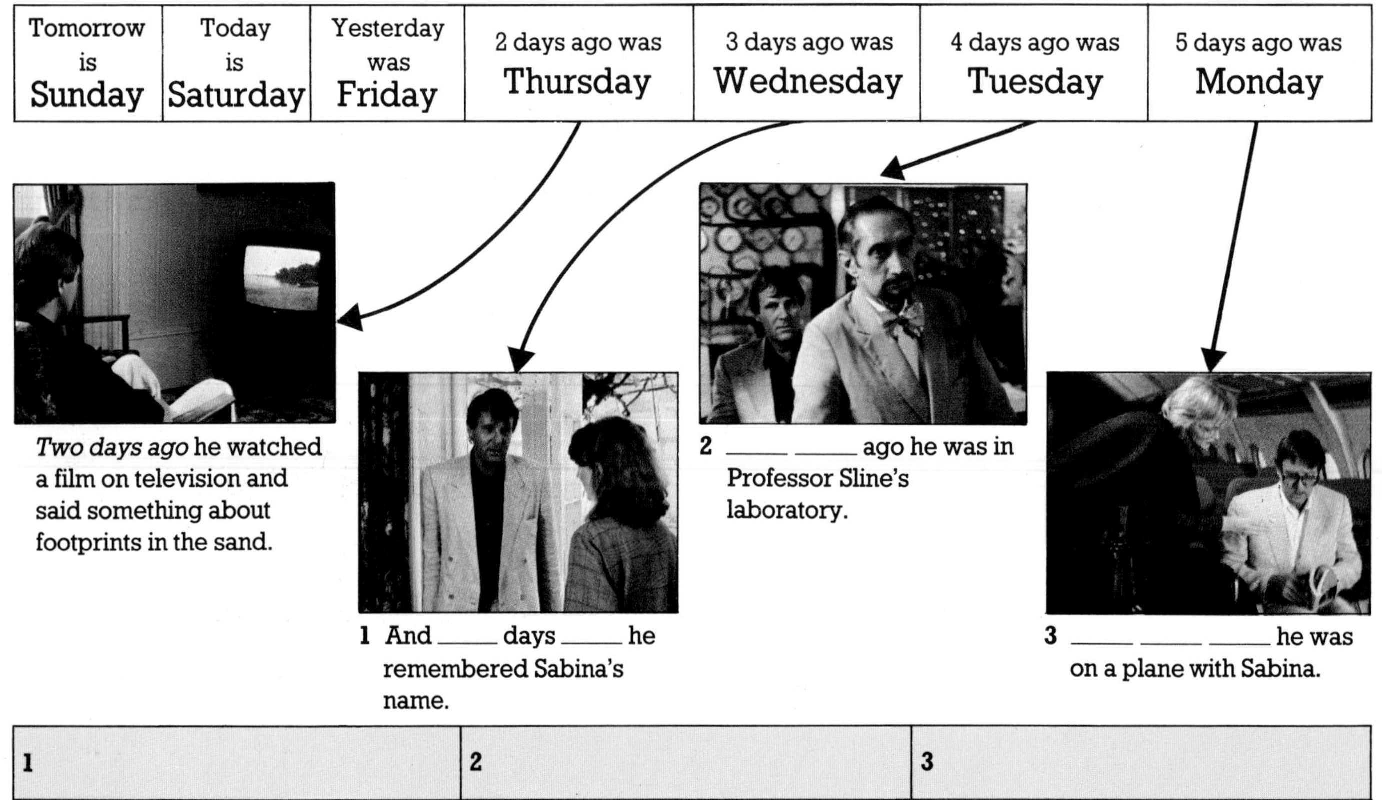

Tomorrow is Sunday	Today is Saturday	Yesterday was Friday	2 days ago was Thursday	3 days ago was Wednesday	4 days ago was Tuesday	5 days ago was Monday

Two days ago he watched a film on television and said something about footprints in the sand.

1 And _____ days _____ he remembered Sabina's name.

2 _____ _____ ago he was in Professor Sline's laboratory.

3 _____ _____ _____ he was on a plane with Sabina.

1	**2**	**3**

Focus Two

I'll _____.

Find the right sentence for each picture.

a) I'll take that one.
b) I'll see you tomorrow at twelve thirty.
c) I'll answer it.
d) Don't worry! I'll help you.

1	**2**	**3**	**4**

Focus Three

Do/Would you like ______?

Find the right question for each picture.

a) Would you like a lift?
b) Do you like orange juice?
c) Do you like rain?
d) Would you like a cup of tea?

1	2	3	4

Focus Four

Why ______? Because ______.

Find the right answer to each question.

a) Because it's early.
b) Because I'm busy.
c) Because the traffic was heavy.
d) Because I'm hungry.

1	2	3	4

Unit 5

Review

1 Complete this summary of episode 5. Find the right words.

When the phone rang, Orwell 1__________ (is/was) asleep.
It was 2__________ (early/late) in the 3__________ (morning/evening).
'Can you 4__________ (look/see) your manuscript?' Sline asked.
Then he 5__________ (gives/gave) Orwell the 6__________ (name/number) of an Italian restaurant. When Orwell got to Alfredo's,
Sabina was there, 7__________ (and/but) Sline wasn't.
Sabina 8__________ (ordered/asked) orange juice and lasagne.
Then Sline 9__________ (arrives/arrived). He was late 10__________ (why/because) the traffic was heavy. 11__________ (Sabina/Orwell) was angry.
'Where's my manuscript?' 12__________ (he/she) said.
Suddenly Orwell began to feel very 13__________ (ill/well).
14__________ (It/There) was something wrong 15__________ (in/with) him.
Sline said, '16__________ (We/You) understand 17__________ (our/your) problem.'

2 Look at this map.

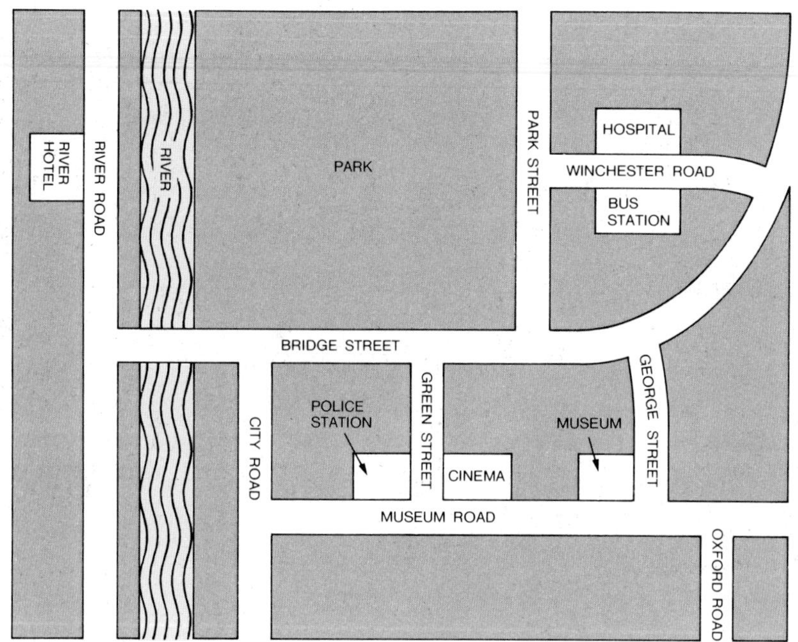

a) You are in the River Hotel. A woman asks you, 'Excuse me, how do I get to the cinema?' What do you say?

b) You went to the cinema yesterday. Suddenly you began to feel very ill, so you walked to the hospital. How did you get there?

3 Find the right words for the questions (1–8).

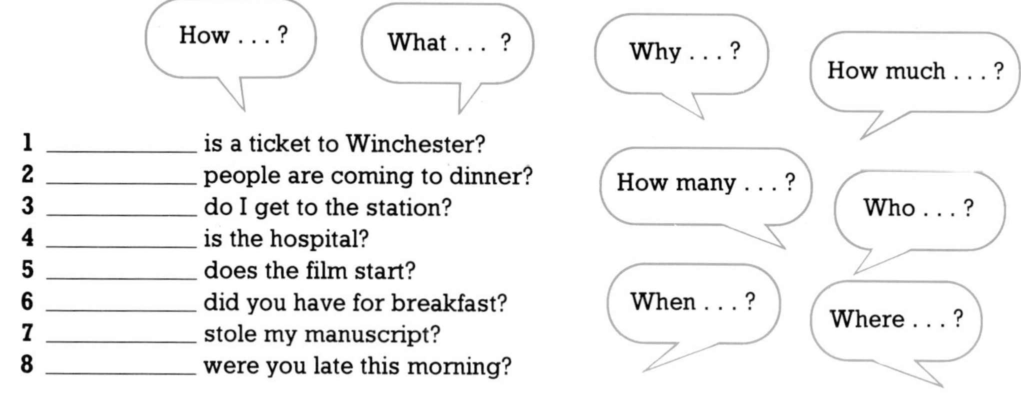

1 __________ is a ticket to Winchester?
2 __________ people are coming to dinner?
3 __________ do I get to the station?
4 __________ is the hospital?
5 __________ does the film start?
6 __________ did you have for breakfast?
7 __________ stole my manuscript?
8 __________ were you late this morning?

Unit 6

THE LABORATORY

Preview

1 Look at the pictures. What can you remember about the other episodes?

1 This man stood on a bridge in episode 1. What did he say? What did he do?
2 The inspector asked some questions. What were they? Did the man answer them?
3 Where did he meet her? He asked her some questions. What were they? What were her answers?
4 What did the man have with him at the airport? Where was it? What did the customs officer ask?
5 What was in front of him when he phoned? What did he say to Orwell?
6 What did she say to Orwell when he came into the restaurant? What did she order? What happened then?

Exercise 1

Before you watch, look at this picture and answer the questions. What do you think?

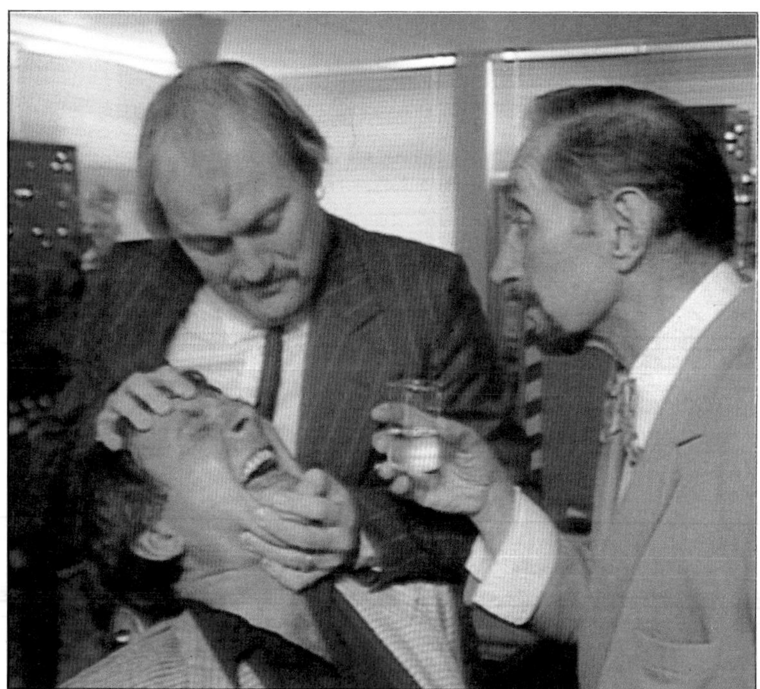

1 Where are they?
2 How did Orwell get there?
3 What are Sline and Harry going to do?
4 What is in the glass?
5 What will happen to Orwell?

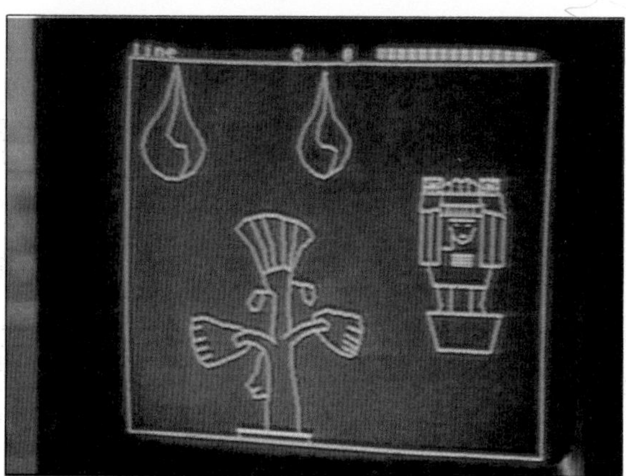

Now look at this picture. You are going to see these symbols in episode 6.

6 Where do you think they come from?
7 What do you think they mean?

Exercise 2

Look at these words (1–10). Find the connections (a–j).

1 language	a) angry
2 argument	b) flame
3 kill	c) water
4 burn	d) plant
5 thirsty	e) English
6 flower	f) dead
7 terrible	g) February
8 laboratory	h) play
9 month	i) scientist
10 toy	j) bad

1	2	3	4	5	6	7	8	9	10

63.16
75.38

Now watch episode 6. Then do exercises 3 and 4.

Exercise 3

Did it happen (Y) or didn't it happen (N)?

1 Orwell and Sline came out of the restaurant.
2 They got on a bus.
3 Sline took Orwell to a hospital.
4 He took him to his laboratory.
5 He asked him a lot of questions.
6 He gave him a glass of water.
7 Orwell wanted something to drink.
8 Sline showed him some strange symbols.
9 He gave Orwell something to drink, but it wasn't a glass of water.
10 Sabina destroyed Orwell's manuscript.
11 She said they didn't want to destroy it.
12 Sline wanted to kill her.
13 He wanted to kill Orwell.
14 Sabina and Sline had an argument.
15 Harry showed Sline a game.

1	2	3	4	5	6	7	8

9	10	11	12	13	14	15

Exercise 4

There are a few things wrong with this story. Can you find them?

The Lost Secret

There was a car outside the restaurant. Orwell felt terrible and didn't know why. He looked at the driver. There was something wrong with the man's head.

Sline and Orwell got in the back of the car. Sabina sat in front, next to Harry.

"Where to, boss?" Harry asked.

"Don't ask stupid questions!" Sline told him. Then he looked at Sabina. "I hope he's going to be all right. How many tablets did you give him?" he asked her.

"Half a tablet. That's what you said," she answered.

"I know what I said! And I said a whole tablet!" Sline said. He looked at Harry again.

"Why are you driving so fast? Don't drive fast. Drive slowly," he said.

"All right, boss. I'll drive faster," Harry said.

If you aren't sure what is wrong, look at this part of the episode again and find out.

65.21
67.01

But what happened when they got to Sline's laboratory? Do you remember this part? Read the cartoon strip and then answer the questions below.

Exercise 5

What is the best alternative?

Example: I need a drink.

a) Give me some money.
b) Give me some food.
✓**c**) Give me some water.

1 I'm thirsty.
a) I'd like some food.
b) I'd like some water.
c) I'd like something to eat.

2 I'm going to ask you just a few questions.
a) . . . one or two or perhaps three questions.
b) . . . 10 or 20 or 30 or more questions.
c) . . . one question.

3 I want to show you something.
a) Answer this question.
b) Drink this.
c) Look at this.

4 turn it on
a) turn it to the left
b) I want to watch it (or listen to it)
c) turn it to the right

1	2	3	4

What happened then? How much did you understand? Do exercise 6 and find out.

67.02
69.15

Exercise 6

1 Find the right answer.

a) They are going to get Orwell a glass of water.
b) They say they are going to destroy the manuscript and photographs.
c) Sline is going to destroy Orwell.
d) Sline is going to destroy Harry.

2 Find the right answer.

a) Because Sline doesn't like Orwell's manuscript.
b) Because Sline can't answer Orwell's questions.
c) Because Orwell doesn't want to answer Sline's questions.
d) Because Sline doesn't understand Orwell's manuscript.

3 Find the right answer.

a) The symbol doesn't mean anything.
b) Orwell doesn't know what it means.
c) Does Orwell know what it means? Sline wants to find out.
d) The symbol means 'destroy'.

4 What does Sline's answer mean?

a) Are you telling the truth? I want to find out.
b) I know you're telling the truth.
c) I know you aren't telling the truth.
d) Am I telling the truth? Do you want to find out?

1	2	3	4

Exercise 7

Again there are a few things wrong with the story. Can you find them?

The Lost Secret

Orwell didn't want to answer Sline's questions about the two symbols for 'rain' and 'flower'. Then Sabina spoke to him.

"The two together mean 'rainflower', don't they, Dr Orwell?" she asked.

"Sabina, we already know that," Sline said. He turned back to the computer and pressed a button. The computer showed a strange symbol. Orwell looked at it.

"This symbol here. Does it mean 'man' or 'woman'?" Sline asked.

"I don't know," Orwell answered. But Sline didn't believe him.

"You don't know," he said slowly. Then he looked at Harry.

Harry held the manuscript and the photographs over the flame again, but Sabina stopped him.

"Please, Dr Orwell, we don't want to destroy your manuscript. All that work. Years of your life. I know how important it is. Go on, tell him."

The Lost Secret

Orwell looked at Sline again.

"I don't know. Really I don't. Perhaps it means 'rain', perhaps it means 'flower' . . . or perhaps it means 'person'."

Sline listened. Then he smiled. It wasn't a nice smile.

"You know, Dr Orwell, I don't need your help at all. Yes, you know a lot, but I know more. So I don't need you," he said. He looked at Harry again and told him to bring the drug.

"Drug? What drug?" Orwell asked.

"The Mepatecs made a drug. It destroyed the memory. They made it from the Telo plant. A North American plant. Now I'm going to test the drug, and you're going to help me."

He looked at Harry. Harry held Orwell's arms and legs. "Does it really destroy the memory, Dr Orwell? I'm going to find out. And Sabina is going to help me," he said.

If you aren't sure what is wrong, perhaps these questions will help you.

1 What did the strange symbol really mean?
2 What did Harry do when Sline gave Orwell the drug?
3 What did Sline say before he gave Orwell the drug?

If you still aren't sure what is wrong with the story, you can also look at this part of the episode again.

Exercise 8

Can you put Dr Roberts' questions and Orwell's answers in the right order?

a) 'Tell me about it. Tell me what happened,' she said.
b) 'Who? Sabina?'
c) 'What happened then? What did he do?' Dr Roberts asked Orwell.
d) 'Yes,' Orwell said. 'She stopped him. And then they had an argument.'
e) 'She stopped him,' he answered.

1 C	2	3	4	5

71.48
72.48

Exercise 9

What are the missing words? Write them in the boxes below.

Stop! You shouldn't do it. Not yet. It's too soon.
You don't know what you're talking about.
You don't know enough about the drug. We need more __1__.
I know enough!
You can't be sure. You still __2__ him. Perhaps he can give you more information.
More? More __3__ what?
Where you can find more Telo plants.
That's no problem. I can get more Telo plants.
But where?
We'll find out __4__.
You should find out now! You __5__ give him the drug until...
That's enough!
But you can't...
__6__!
Look at him. Do you __7__ to kill him?
Yes! But the memory drug won't __8__ him! Don't worry about that! No, I have other ideas for that. But I'm still not sure how I'm __9__ to __10__ it.

1 information	2	3	4	5
6	7	8	9	10

Exercise 10

Look at the cartoon and then read the story below. What's wrong with it?

The Lost Secret

Sline stood there, thinking. Just then he heard a strange noise. It came from the other end of the room. Harry was there. He had something in his hands.

"Harry! What are you doing?" Sline said.

Harry looked at him. He was afraid.

"Nothing, boss."

"What was that noise?" Sline asked. Harry didn't want to answer. Sline saw the game in his hands. It was a computer game, the kind children play with.

"Give it to me. Another stupid toy! What is it this time?" he shouted. He took the toy from Harry's hands and looked at it. Then he suddenly stopped. He was suddenly very interested in it. Harry began to tell him about it.

"You press this button here, and then you press this one here, and a little bird flies through the air . . ."

Suddenly Sline had an idea.

"A bird. Of course, that's how I'm going to do it. Birds can fly, but people can't."

He pointed to the toy.

"Bring that here!" he shouted.

Harry gave him the toy. Sline looked at it again and told Harry to hold Orwell's head. Then he put the toy in his mouth.

Look at this part of the episode again if you aren't sure what is wrong.

75.07
75.38

Exercise 11

Watch the last part of the episode again. Then put the parts of the story below in the right order.

a) Then she showed Marvin a picture.
Marvin looked at it and then said, "I'm not sure. I know they gave him a drug."
The man looked at Marvin. He was very interested.

b) "Dr Roberts thinks it was a memory drug," Marvin answered.
"What do you mean?" the woman asked.

c) The man and the woman looked at Marvin.
Then the man said, "Listen, Inspector, we want to know more about this drug. It's important, very important!"

d) "What kind of drug?" he asked.

e) "Now, there's something we want to ask you, Inspector," the man said.
"Yes?" Marvin said.
"Why is Sline interested in this man?" the woman asked.

f) "It destroys the memory," Marvin replied.

1	2	3	4	5	6

Exercise 12

Find the best explanation.

1 interested in
a) like something
b) not like something
c) want to learn more about something

2 drug
a) something to eat
b) something like heroin, opium, morphine
c) a symbol or word from a strange language

1	2

What do you think?

Do you think the man and the woman are Sline's friends?
Are they Orwell's friends?
Why do they want to know more about the drug?
Why were they in the restaurant when Orwell met Sabina and Sline?

Focus One

going to

Find the right sentence for each picture.

a) He's going to jump
b) It's going to rain.
c) We're going to steal some money.
d) I'm going to eat all this.

1	2	3	4

Focus Two

taller/shorter/faster/bigger

Is the right word **a)** or **b)**?

For example:

The man is tall, but the woman is taller.
The woman is taller than the man.

1 The woman is **a)** shorter / **b)** short

2 ... but the man is **a)** short. / **b)** shorter.

3 A car is **a)** fast / **b)** faster

4 ... but an aeroplane is **a)** faster. / **b)** fast.

5 Is a car **a)** fast / **b)** faster than an aeroplane?

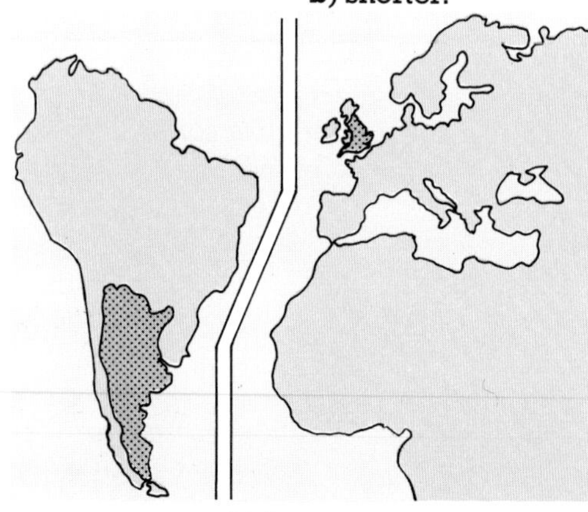

6 Is Argentina **a)** bigger / **b)** big than England?

1	2	3	4	5	6

Focus Three

should/shouldn't

Find the right sentence for each picture.

a) You should always tell the truth.
b) You shouldn't drive fast in traffic.
c) You should see a doctor.
d) You shouldn't steal things.

1	2	3	4

Focus Four

Parts of the body

Find the words for the parts of the body.

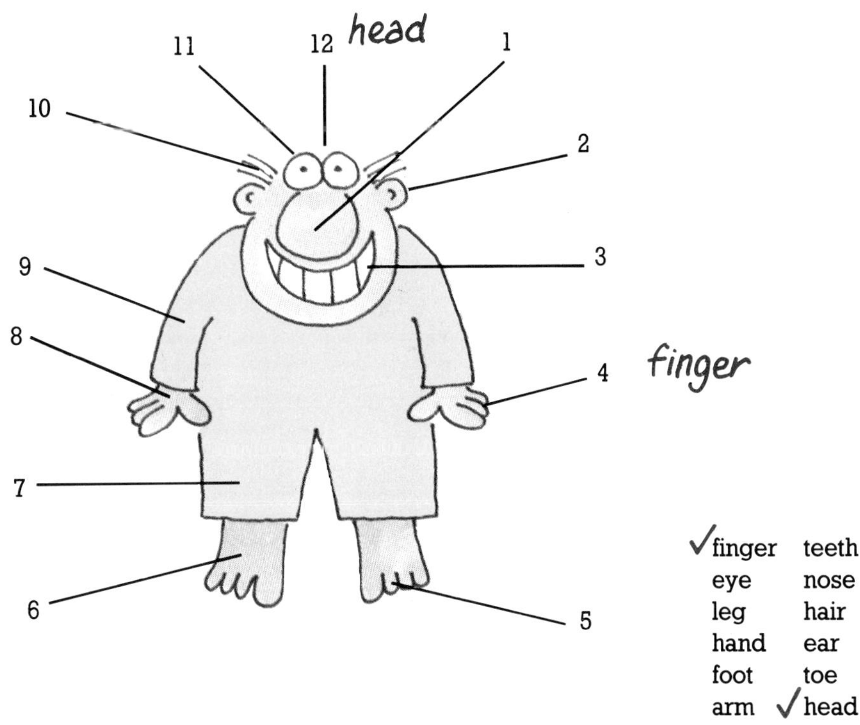

✓finger	teeth
eye	nose
leg	hair
hand	ear
foot	toe
arm	✓head

Unit 6

Review

1 These things happened to Dr Orwell (a–f). Put them in the right order (1–6).

a) He remembered Sabina's name.
b) Inspector Marvin asked him some questions at a police station.
c) He told Dr Roberts about a lost civilisation called the Mepatecs.
d) He stood on a bridge and said, 'I'm a bird. I can fly.'
e) Then Dr Roberts asked him some questions at a clinic.
f) He remembered his name too.

2 Dr Orwell remembered these things (a–f). Put them in the right order (1–6).

a) He felt very ill.
b) Professor Sline telephoned him.
c) She introduced him to Professor Sline.
d) He met Sabina in a restaurant.
e) He met Sabina on an aeroplane.
f) He checked in to his hotel.

3 Now finish these sentences about the Mepatecs.

The Mepatecs 1__________ an old civilisation in 2__________ America. They disappeared about fifteen hundred years 3__________. They 4__________ a drug from the Telo plant. It 5__________ a very dangerous drug because it 6__________ the memory.

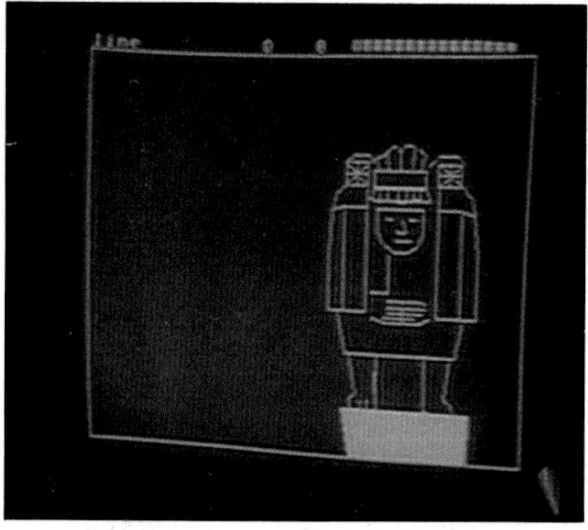

This is a symbol from the Mepatec 7__________.
What does it 8__________? Man, 9__________ or person?
Nobody 10__________.

4 Test. Complete these sentences. Then answer the questions.

1 What are you __________ to do on Saturday?
2 Do you think it __________ going to rain tomorrow?
3 How old do you think Orwell is? Is he older or __________ than you?
4 Are you thirsty? __________ you like some water?
5 What about some food? Are you __________ ?
6 What __________ you do yesterday?
7 Are you interested __________ archeology?
8 Do you often go __________ the cinema?
9 Do you usually eat __________ restaurants?
10 Look at page 60. Can you see the Mepatec symbol __________ rain?

Unit 7

GOOD NEWS & BAD NEWS

Preview

1 Can you remember episode 6?

1. Where did they take Orwell after they left the restaurant?
2. Was he really drunk?
3. Professor Sline asked him a few questions. Can you remember any of them?
4. The professor wanted to test something. What?
5. How did he test it?

2 People say these things (1–7) in episode 7. Find good answers (a–g).

1. Can a plant be male or female?
2. Can I help you?
3. What did she look like?
4. There was a page missing.
5. Do you believe him?
6. Did you see her too?
7. How long will that take?

a) She had short blonde hair and was of medium height.
b) A day or two, I think.
c) What a strange question. I don't know. I didn't study botany at school.
d) Yes, I'd like some information, please.
e) Yes, I did.
f) Yes, I do.
g) Where? Which one was it?

3 Here are some important words (1–8) from episode 7. Can you find the opposite words (a–h)?

1 female	**a)** terrible
2 best	**b)** male
3 near	**c)** quickly
4 nearest	**d)** farthest
5 excellent	**e)** far
6 first	**f)** exit
7 entrance	**g)** worst
8 slowly	**h)** last

4 Here are some more things people say. What do you think? Who is speaking? Who are they speaking to? Where are they?

Example: Harry is speaking to Sabina. They are in Professor Sline's laboratory.

Yes, I remember, when I saw her she had a book in her hand.

The boss is waiting for you. And he's angry.

That's the answer. That's why the drug didn't work. And that's the secret. The lost secret! But why didn't I see it?

His memory is coming back, but it's coming back slowly. He can't remember everything.

75:50
88:32

Now watch episode 7. Then do exercises 1, 2 and 3.

Exercise 1

Look at these pictures (1–6). Find a sentence (a–f) to go with each one.

a) 'But how did she get out?' Dr Roberts asked. Then she saw the door.
b) There was a woman at one of the tables. She had short blonde hair.
c) 'Can a plant be male or female?' Orwell asked.
d) He looked up and saw another woman on the balcony.
e) She had some good news for him and some bad news too.
f) They went to the library and asked for some information.

1	2	3	4	5	6

76:10
79:59

Exercise 2

What happened next? Watch this part again. Then put the five parts of the story (a–e) in the right order (1–5).

a) "Excuse me," Dr Roberts said. The man didn't answer.
"Excuse me!" she said again.
"One moment!" the man said. A few seconds later he looked up.
"Yes? Can I help you?" he said.
"I hope so. I'd like some information," she told him.
"You mean you're looking for a book?" he asked.

b) It was a fine, warm day and Orwell and Dr Roberts were in the garden.
"Can a plant be male or female?" he suddenly asked her.
She remembered her botany lessons at school and she knew the answer was "yes". She didn't know how many plants could be male or female but they could find out at the Botanical Institute in Oxford. It had one of the best botanical libraries in the world.

c)

"Why are so many people interested in the Telo plant today?"

Orwell stopped.

"Pardon? What did you say about the Telo plant?"

"Somebody else was here trying to get information on the Telo plant. She was here a few minutes ago," the man said. Then he described the woman. She was of medium height, with short blonde hair.

Orwell walked over to the books. Suddenly he stopped. There was a woman with a book in front of her at one of the tables. He couldn't see her face, but he could see that she had short blonde hair.

"Sabina!" Orwell said.

d)

Orwell said he wanted a book about the Telo plant. At first the man didn't understand. Then he told him it was "over there, in the South American section". Dr Roberts wanted to make a telephone call. The nearest public telephone was a call box outside the library, near the entrance.

"I'll meet you over there in a minute," she said, and left. Orwell began to walk over to the South American section when he heard the man say something to the other man at the desk.

e)

"Let's go there," Orwell said.

"Tomorrow?"

"No, today! Let's go there now! This afternoon. It's very important!" he told her.

She asked why.

"I think I know why the drug didn't work!" Orwell answered.

It took them about two hours to get to Oxford. They drove there in her car. The library and the institute were in an old building near the centre of the town. The man at the front desk was busy and didn't look up when Orwell and Dr Roberts came in.

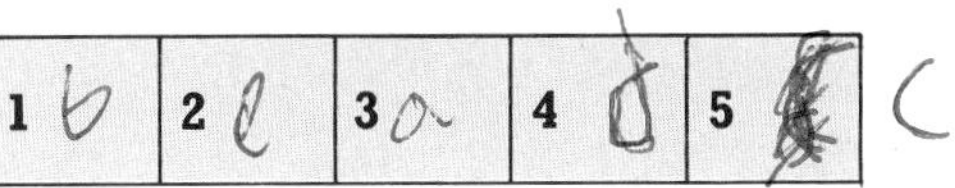

1	2	3	4	5

Exercise 3

Find the phrase closest in meaning.

1 Let's go there.
a) I want to go there. Please come with me.
b) I don't want to go there now.
c) I don't think we should go there.

2 You mean you're looking for a book?
a) You think you are reading a book.
b) Do you want to read a book?
c) Do you want to find a book?

3 He described the woman.
a) He didn't like her.
b) He said what she looked like.
c) He thought he knew her.

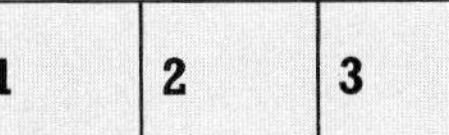

1	2	3

80:30
81:20

Exercise 4

Look at Dr Roberts' questions (1–4). Find Orwell's answers (a–d).

1 What's wrong?
2 Who? Who did you see?
3 Who was on the balcony? Who are you talking about?
4 Yes? What happened then?

a) Did I see her? Or didn't I?
b) Sabina! She was there. She saw me and . . . and then . . .
c) I'm not sure, but I think I saw her.
d) She was up there. Up there on the balcony.

1	2	3	4 a

81:10
82:18

Exercise 5

What happened next? Watch this part again. Then put the pictures (a–h) in the right order.

a) 

b) 

c) 

d) 

e) 

f) 

g) 

h) 

1	2	3	4
5	6	7	8

82:20
84:15

Watch this part again and read the cartoon strip. Then do exercises 6 and 7.

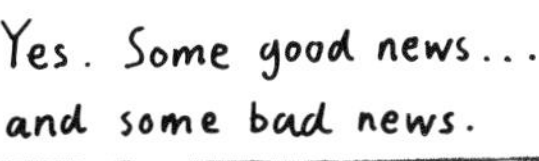

Exercise 6

What does it mean? Excellent!

a) Very good!
b) Very bad!
c) Very strange!

Exercise 7

True or false?

1 Sabina didn't go to the library.
2 The good news is that there are Telo plants growing in England.
3 Sabina gave Sline the bad news before she gave him the good news.
4 She is going to give him the bad news now.

1	2	3	4

84:18
86:32

Now watch this part again. Then do exercise 8.

Exercise 8

There are a few things wrong with the story. Can you find them?

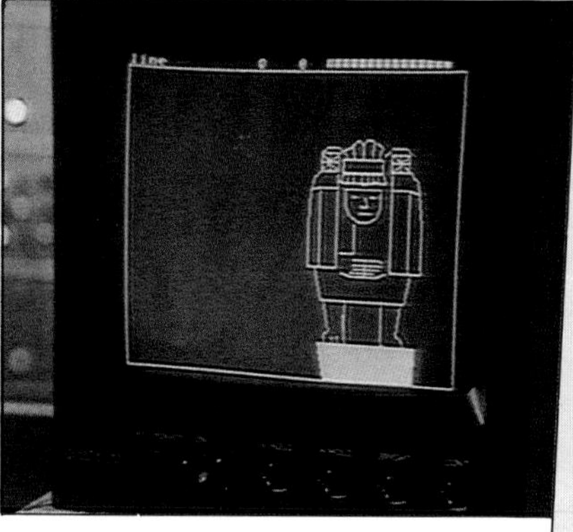

The Lost Secret

"I saw Dr Orwell at the library," Sabina told Sline. He looked at her. There was still a smile on his face.

"Orwell? But he's dead," he said.

"No, he isn't," Sabina answered.

Sline turned and shouted, "Harry!"

Harry looked at him. He was afraid.

"And he remembered my name," Sabina said.

"But the memory drug . . . " Sline began.

"The drug didn't work! Perhaps you should listen to me sometimes, Basil," Sabina told him.

Sline didn't say anything for a moment.

"I have to . . . think about this. Get me Orwell's manuscript. You know where I keep it," he said.

Harry brought the manuscript. Sabina pressed some buttons on the computer.

"What does he say about this symbol?" Sline asked Sabina.

"It's somewhere near the end, I think. Yes, here it is. Look!" she answered, and pointed to a symbol in the

The Lost Secret

manuscript. She pressed some more buttons on the computer.

The computer showed a symbol. This first symbol was the symbol for the word 'rain'. Then it showed another symbol. The second symbol meant 'flower'. Then the computer showed a third symbol.

"This one means 'person'," Sline said.

Sabina looked at him.

"Orwell didn't know about that symbol. He wasn't sure. Don't you remember? Perhaps it means 'woman', perhaps it means 'man'," she told him.

Suddenly Sline stopped. He said the three words again.

"'Man' or 'woman'. . . or 'person'."

There was a strange look on his face.

"But of course! That's the answer. That's why the drug didn't work. And that's the secret. The lost secret! But why didn't I see it? Why didn't I understand?" he said slowly.

"What secret? What are you talking about?" Sabina asked.

Sline told her.

If you aren't sure what is wrong, perhaps these questions will help you.

1 Who brought Sline the manuscript?
2 Who pressed the buttons on the computer?
3 What did Sline say when he saw the third symbol?
4 What did Sabina say about the third symbol?
5 What did Sline say to Sabina when she said, 'What secret? What are you talking about?'

86:40
87:37

Now watch this part again.

Exercise 9

What did Dr Roberts say to Inspector Marvin later? What are the missing words from the conversation below?

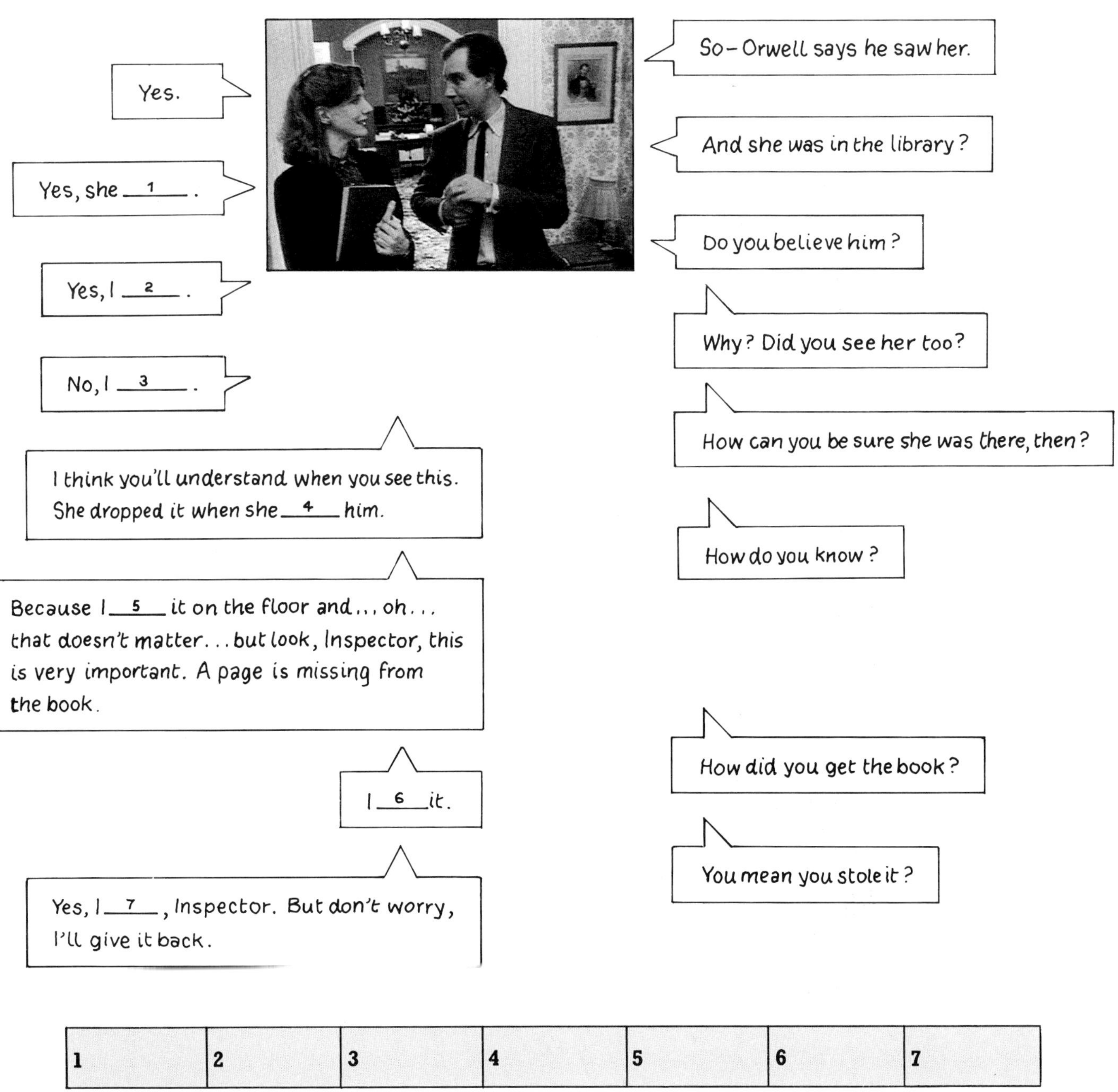

1	2	3	4	5	6	7

Exercise 10

Find the right word for each sentence below: *does, doesn't, did* or *didn't*?

1 Does Dr Roberts believe Orwell?
Yes, she ______ .

2 Did she see Sabina too?
No, she ______ .

3 Did she take a book from the library?
Yes, she ______ .

4 Does she want to keep the book?
No, she ______ .

1	2	3	4

87:38
88:14

Now watch this part again. Then do exercises 11, 12 and 13.

Exercise 11

Can you remember the missing words? Write them in the boxes.

All right. But remember, Inspector, he's tired. His memory is coming back, but it's coming back 8. He can't remember 9. Don't ask him any 10 questions – not at first. Go slowly!

1	2	3	4	5
6	7	8	9	10

Exercise 12

What does it mean?

1 missing
a) first
b) lost
c) interesting

2 copy
a) another book with the same things in it
b) a book with more pictures
c) a shorter book

3 His memory is coming back slowly.
a) He can remember some things again.
b) He can't remember anything.
c) He can remember everything.

1	2	3

Exercise 13

Find the right word for each sentence below: *is, isn't, can* or *can't*?

1 Can they get another copy of the book?
Yes, they ______.

2 Can Marvin get a copy of the book today?
No, he ______.

3 Is he going to ask Orwell a lot of questions?
No, he ______.

4 Is he going to ask Orwell a few questions?
Yes, he ______.

1	2	3	4

88:14
88:32

Exercise 14

Watch this part again. Then find the other two mistakes in the dialogue.

Alice: Get closer. I can't hear what they're thinking. saying

George: He's a good driver! I don't want to get too close.

Alice: I have to hear what they're saying! I know they're going to Brighton.

Exercise 15

What do you think it means?

I have to hear what they're saying!

a) I can't hear what they're saying.
b) I want to hear what they're saying. It's important!
c) I can hear what they're saying.

Exercise 16

Which word doesn't belong?

1 good nice terrible fine
2 lost missing here can't find
3 thing man woman person
4 book page words game
5 look listen watch see
6 speak talk say look
7 a lot a few some not many
8 minute hour time drug

Exercise 17

Make a word from the letters.

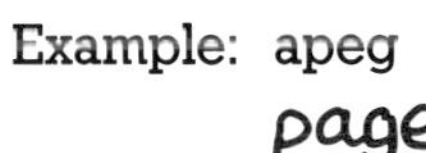

Example: apeg page

1 lema

2 mefale

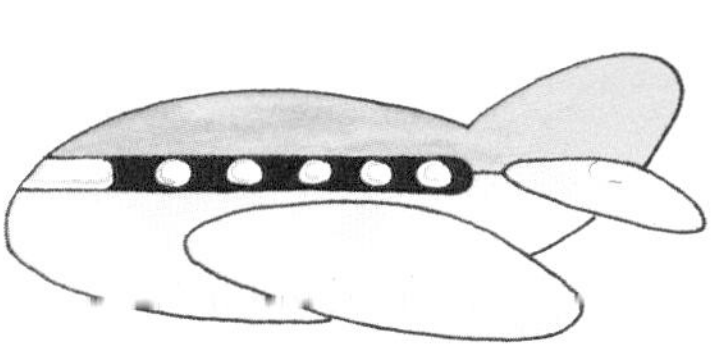

3 paraneleo

4 cholso

5 rilaybr

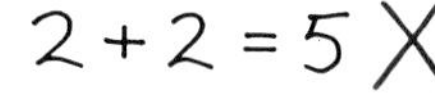

6 simatek

1	2	3
4	5	6

Focus One

How do they feel?

Find a sentence (a–i) for each picture (1–9).

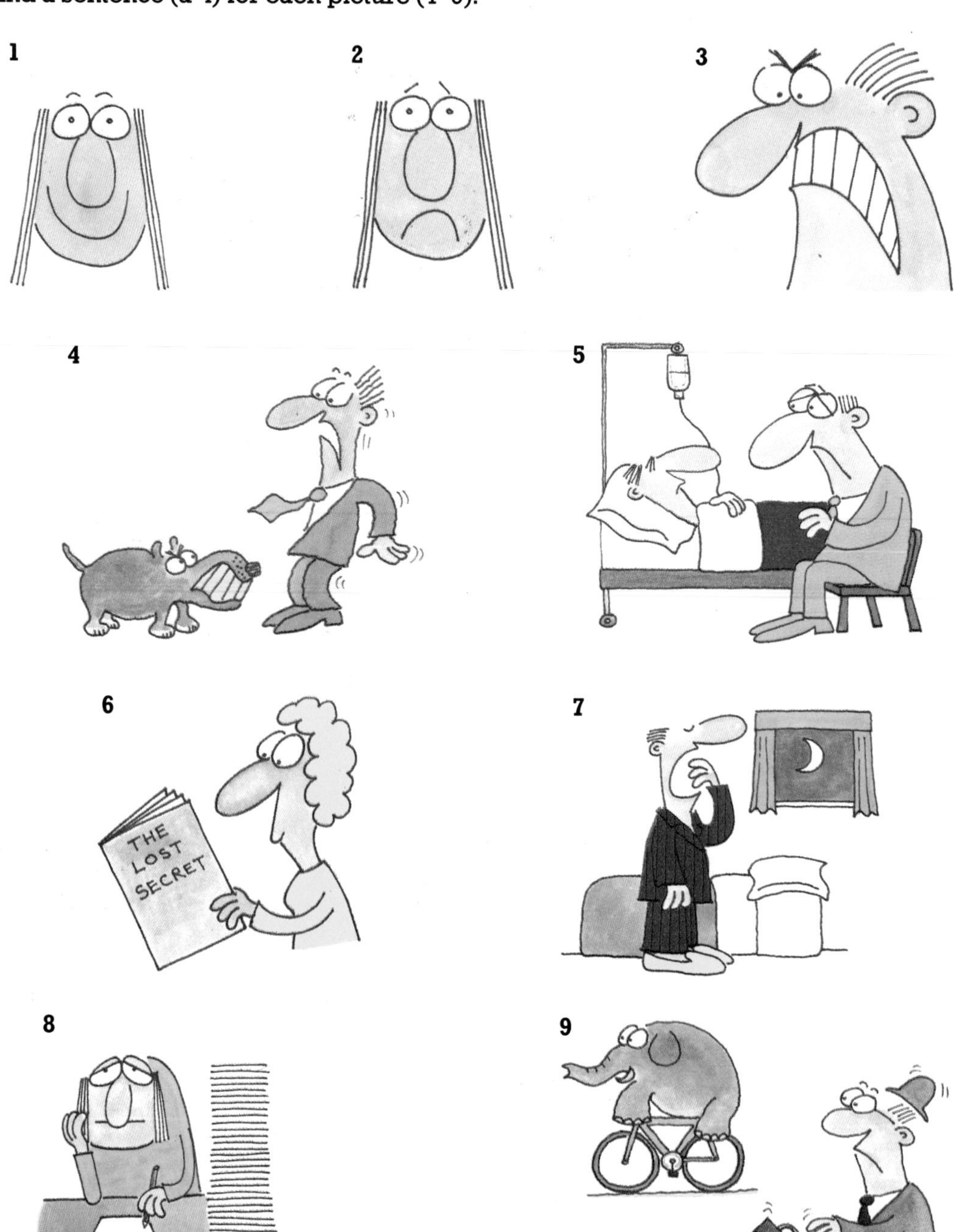

a) He's tired. It's late and it's time for bed.
b) He's worried because his father is very ill.
c) She's very interested in the book. It's a very interesting story.
d) She's very bored. She has a lot of work to do and it isn't very interesting.
e) She's sad because she had some very bad news yesterday.
f) She's happy because she had some very good news yesterday.
g) He's very surprised. He just can't believe it! An elephant on a bicycle!
h) He's very, very angry because someone stole his car.
i) He's afraid of that dog. Just look at those big teeth!

1	2	3	4	5	6	7	8	9

Focus Two

Let's ______.

What do you think the other person is saying? Find an answer (a–f) for each picture (1–6).

a) That's a good idea. I'm hungry.
b) All right. I'll make some.
c) Come on! We'll be there soon.
d) We can't. There's something wrong with it.
e) All right. Which film would you like to see?
f) No, it isn't. It's early.

1	2	3	4	5	6

Focus Three

too

Find the right answer (a–d) for the questions (1–4).

1 What's wrong with the jacket?

2 Why can't she get the book?

3 Is he going to buy the television?

4 Why doesn't she like the weather?

a) No, it's too expensive.
b) Because it's too hot.
c) It's too big for him.
d) Because she's too short.

1	2	3	4

Unit 7

Review

1 Complete this summary of episode 7.

Dr Orwell 1__________ in a garden with Dr Roberts when he 2__________ some flowers.
'Can a plant be male or 3__________ ?' he asked.
'Yes, some plants can be 4__________ or 5__________ ,' Dr Roberts answered.

Orwell 6__________ some more information. They went to a 7__________ in Oxford. Dr Roberts had to 8__________ her office. Orwell 9__________ into the library alone. He saw a woman with 10__________ 11__________ hair sitting there. He thought she 12__________ Sabina, but she 13__________ . Then he saw another woman. This time it 14__________ Sabina!

Sabina went back to Sline's 15__________ . She 16__________ some 17__________ news and some good 18__________ . The 19__________ 20 __________ was that she had a page from a book about the Telo plant. The 21__________ 22__________ was that Orwell wasn't dead.

2 Here are some signs (1–6). Can you find the meanings (a–f)?

1

2

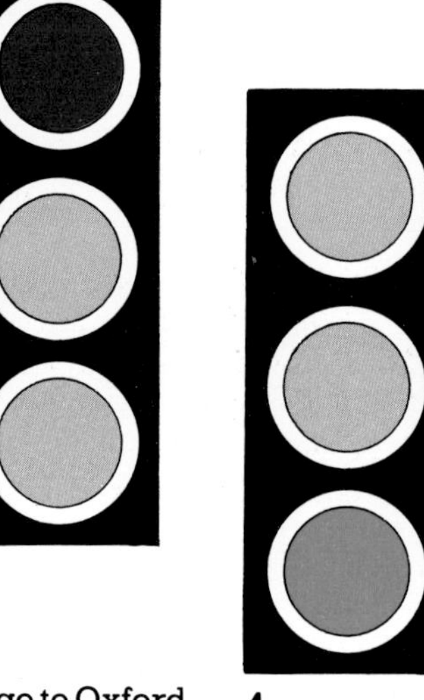

3

4

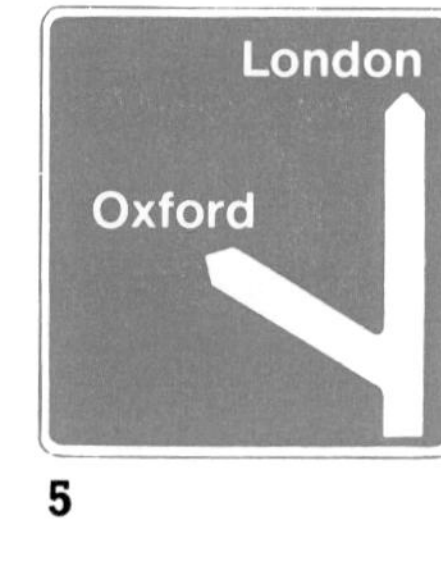

5

6

a) You can go now.
b) Don't go. You have to stop.
c) You have to turn left.
d) You can't turn left.
e) You shouldn't turn left if you want to go to Oxford.
f) You should turn left if you want to go to Oxford.

3 Here are some sentences about episode 7. They are all false. Write true sentences.

Example: Orwell was sure he saw Sabina.
No, he wasn't sure he saw her.

1 The drug worked. It destroyed Orwell's memory.
2 The man in the library gave them a lot of information about the Telo plant.
3 Sabina spoke to Orwell.
4 She was in the library when Dr Roberts came back.
5 Dr Roberts saw her too.
6 The missing page from the book was on the floor.
7 Sabina gave Professor Sline the bad news first.
8 Sabina knew what the lost secret was.

Unit 8

MALE & FEMALE

Preview

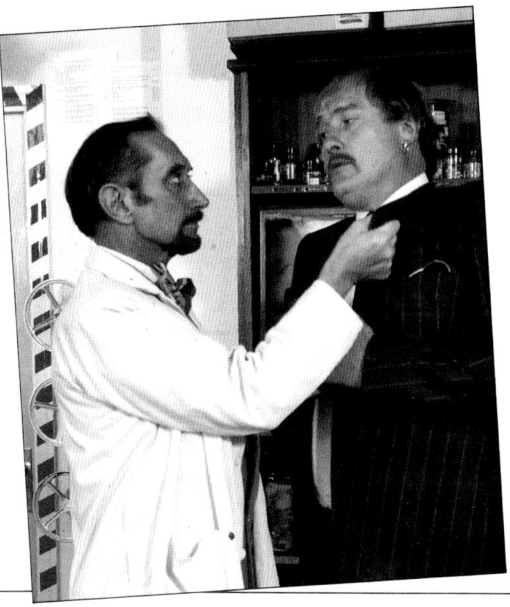

1 Can you remember episode 7?

1 Why was Professor Sline angry with Harry?
2 What was the bad news?
3 Who gave Sline the bad news?
4 What was the good news?
5 Where did Sabina get the good news?

2 Here are some things people say in episode 8. Can you match the sentences (1–4) with the descriptions (a–d)?

1 He was interested in the memory drug. He wanted to know how to make it.
2 People will pay us for this secret.
3 You're losing them! You're losing them!
4 There was something wrong with it. Why didn't it work?

a) Alice is talking to George about Sline, Sabina and Harry.
b) Sabina is talking to Sline about the memory drug.
c) Orwell is talking to Inspector Marvin about Sline.
d) Sline is talking to Sabina about the memory drug.

Here are four more things people say. Can you guess what they are talking about?

Well, go on! What does it say? Where do they grow in England?

They're here! I've found them!

Sabina took it. Look!

They said it looked like water. No colour, no taste, but with a strange smell.

3 Here are some important words (1–8) from episode 8. Can you find the opposite words (a–h)?

1 empty
2 lose
3 impossible
4 strong
5 careful
6 stupid
7 turn on
8 expensive

a) possible
b) careless
c) full
d) cheap
e) weak
f) turn off
g) find
h) intelligent

88:42
100:52

Watch episode 8. Then do exercise 1.

Exercise 1

True or false?

1) Sline thinks he can make a lot of money.
2) He needs a male and a female Telo plant.
3) He can get these plants only in South America.
4) Orwell doesn't think the news on television is interesting.

1	2	3	4

89:03
90:07

Now read this part of the story. Then do exercise 2.

The Lost Secret

"Have you seen this man before?" Inspector Marvin asked. He showed Orwell a photograph.

"Of course I have. It's Sline," Orwell answered.

"And have you seen this woman before?" the inspector asked, showing him another photograph.

"Yes. It's Sabina," Orwell told him.

The inspector pointed to the first photograph.

"Did this man steal your manuscript?"

"Yes, he did. He's still got it," Orwell answered.

Marvin looked at him carefully.

"But why did he steal it?" he asked.

"He wanted to understand the Mepatecs' language. He was interested in their memory drug. He wanted to know how to make it," Orwell said.

The inspector didn't say anything for a moment. Then he asked his next question.

"Do you know how to make the drug?"

"No, I don't."

The inspector looked at him very carefully.

"Did you want to make it, Dr Orwell?" he asked slowly.

"No, I didn't," Orwell said. He stood up. He was angry. He didn't want to answer any more questions.

Exercise 2

What is the right answer: **a**), **b**) or **c**)?

1 Who is the person in the first photograph?
a) Sabina
b) Sline
c) Inspector Marvin

2 Who is the person in the second photograph?
a) Sabina
b) Sline
c) Dr Roberts

3 Did Orwell want to make the drug?
a) Yes.
b) No.
c) He doesn't answer the question.

4 Does Inspector Marvin believe Orwell?
a) Yes.
b) No.
c) We don't know.

1	2	3	4

90:07
91:44

Now watch this part again. Then do exercises 3, 4 and 5.

Exercise 3

What are the missing words?

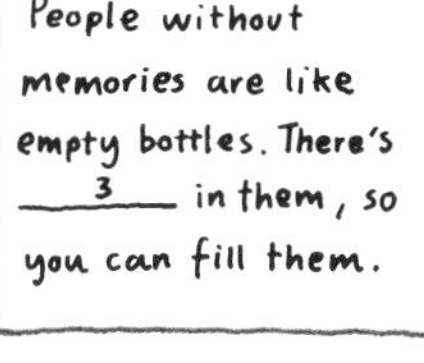

1	2	3	4	5	6	7	8

Exercise 4

What did they say then: **a**), **b**) or **c**)?

1 **Sabina:** Ten years ago, when we first ______, you wanted to control me, didn't you?
a) met
b) meet
c) are meeting

2 **Sline:** Control you? My dear Sabina, I wanted to help you. And you needed my help. Because you wanted money. You ______ money
a) loves
b) love
c) loved

3 **Sline:** Don't you worry! People will pay ______ for this drug, for this secret.
a) me
b) you
c) us

4 **Sabina:** People? ______
a) What?
b) Who?
c) Where?

1	2	3	4

Exercise 5

What does it mean: **a**), **b**) or **c**)?

1 People without memories are like empty bottles.
a) When people lose their memories, they like bottles with nothing in them.
b) People can lose their memories when they drink a lot.
c) When people lose their memories you can say they are 'empty bottles' because they can't remember anything.

2 You want to control people.
You want to . . .
a) look in their pockets.
b) tell people things and then they will do what you say.
c) tell people things and they will always remember them.

1	2

91:45
92:09

Watch this part again. Then do exercises 6 and 7.

Exercise 6

Where do these words go?

a) see **b)** hear **c)** know **d)** driver **e)** driving

You're losing them! You're losing them!

I know I'm losing them, but he's going too fast. He's a terrible __1__.

I can't __2__ them now!

I can't __3__ them now! Where are they?

I don't __4__!

It's impossible. He's __5__ too fast!

1	2	3	4	5

Exercise 7

What do you think is the right answer: **a**), **b**) or **c**)?

1 Who are they talking about?
a) Orwell
b) Inspector Marvin
c) Sline, Sabina and Harry

2 Who is a terrible driver?
a) the man with the blond hair
b) Harry
c) we don't know

3 What does the man mean when he says 'It's impossible'?
a) I can't do it!
b) Don't say that!
c) It's terrible!

1	2	3

92:09
93:06

Watch and read this part again. Then do exercises 8 and 9.

The Lost Secret

"So the Mepatecs used the Telo plant to make the memory drug, is that right?" Marvin asked. He was standing behind Orwell.

"Yes," Orwell answered. He didn't look at Marvin.

"And you didn't want to make the drug?"

"No, I didn't."

"Well, why did you bring the Telo plant back to England with you?" Marvin asked.

"It was important for my work, and there are no Telo plants in Europe. It grows only in a few parts of South America," Orwell explained.

The Lost Secret

"That isn't what this book says," Dr Roberts suddenly said. She was sitting near the window and she had a book in her hands. It had a green cover. It was the book from the library. Orwell looked at her. He was very surprised. She stood up and walked over to where Orwell and Marvin were standing.

"Listen," she said. She began to read from the book. "The Telo plant grew well in South America until a thousand years ago. Today there are very few Telo plants in the world. But in England there is one place where they grow."

She stopped. Orwell was looking at her.

"Do you mean there are Telo plants in England too?" he asked.

"That's what the book says."

"Well, go on! What does it say? Where do they grow in England?" Orwell wanted to know. Marvin was still watching him carefully.

"This is the end of the page," Dr Roberts answered.

"Well, read the next page!" Orwell said.

Exercise 8

What happened then? Answer yes or no.

1 Did Dr Roberts read the next page?
2 Was the next page in the book?
3 Did Sabina take the page from the book when she was in the library?

1	2	3

Exercise 9

What does it mean: **a**) or **b**)?

1 The Mepatecs used the Telo plant to make the memory drug.
a) They used the Telo plant. They made the drug with it.
b) They made the drug with the Telo plant a long time ago. They don't make the drug any more.

2 It grew well until a thousand years ago.
a) It grew well a thousand years ago. It still grows well.
b) It grew well. Then it stopped a thousand years ago and doesn't grow well now.

3 Do you mean there are Telo plants in England too?
a) Do you think there are Telo plants in England too?
b) What? There are Telo plants in England too? Is that what you are saying?

1	2	3

93:07
95:39

Now watch this part again. Then do exercises 10 and 11.

Exercise 10

There are 14 missing words in this conversation. What are they?

When you ____1____ the drug on Ross, it didn't work. Why? Have you thought about that?

Of ____2____ I have. It was a small mistake.

A small mistake, Basil? I think it was a big one. A very big one. Orwell isn't ____3____.

He isn't dead ____4____ you didn't do your job! You and this idiot there!

Perhaps we didn't do our job well when we took him to that bridge in Winchester. But the drug ____5____ didn't work. There was something wrong with it. What? Why didn't it work, Basil?

There was one small thing I ____6____ understand.

What? Do you ____7____ my help? Then tell me! Well? Are you going to tell me, or aren't you?

There is a ____8____ Telo plant and a . . .

Go on.

And a female ____9____. Orwell's plant was a male plant. And there was something I didn't know.

What?

You ____10____ to use the male and the female plant to make the drug. One plant isn't ____11____.

You mean the male plant isn't strong enough ____12____ the female plant? And you didn't know that there are male and female plants in this place ____13____ Brighton, did you Basil? Aren't you lucky I'm here to help you, Basil?

No, don't say I'm lucky. Not yet. We have to get the plants first. And that isn't going to be ____14____.

1	2	3	4	5	6	7
8	9	10	11	12	13	14

Exercise 11

True or false?

1 Sline doesn't know why the drug didn't work.
2 He doesn't tell Sabina why the drug didn't work.
3 They can't make a good memory drug with only the male plant.
4 They are going to a place where there are male and female plants.
5 Sline thinks it is going to be easy to get the plants.
6 'Lucky' means having something good happen to you.

1	2	3	4	5	6

95:40
97:52

Now watch this part again. Then read the cartoon strip.

Exercise 12

What happened then: **a**), **b**) or **c**)?

a) Harry put the broken computer in his pocket.
b) He left it in the greenhouse.
c) He left it on the floor.

Now watch this part.

97:53
99:31

Exercise 13

Which word is missing: **a**), **b**) or **c**)?

1 a) Are
b) Is
c) Was

2 a) on
b) under
c) off

3 a) put
b) make
c) turn

4 a) yesterday
b) ago
c) now

5 a) do
b) does
c) is

6 a) like
b) for
c) at

7 a) with
b) of
c) off

8 a) How
b) Why
c) What

1	2	3	4	5	6	7	8

Exercise 14

What does it mean: **a**) or **b**)?

1 What does it look like?
a) Do you like the look of it?
b) Describe it.

2 It looks like water.
a) The taste is as good as water.
b) When you see it you think it is water.

1	2

Exercise 15

What did Orwell say then: **a**) or **b**)?

1 a) There's something I like to ask you.
b) There's something I'd like to ask you.

2 a) And my memory has come back.
b) And my memory came back.

3 a) Why do I have to stay here any longer?
b) Why do I stay here any longer?

4 a) I like to go back to work.
b) I'd like to go back to work.

And what did Dr Roberts say: **a**) or **b**)?

5 a) You mean you like to leave.
b) You mean you'd like to leave.

6 a) I think you should stay for a few more days.
b) I think you will stay for a few more days.

1	2	3	4	5	6

Exercise 16

99:32
100:52

Watch this part of the video. Then read the story.

There are five things wrong with it. Can you find them?

The Lost Secret

"Oh, look! The news has started," Orwell said. They looked at the television and saw a young man in front of a small house.

"This is Norton House, near Brighton. It was the home of the famous botanist Sir Patrick Norton. His house is full of beautiful and expensive things from all over the world. But last night someone broke into the greenhouse and stole some plants. This morning I spoke to Sir Patrick Norton's granddaughter," the reporter said.

Then Orwell and Dr Roberts saw the reporter with another person outside a greenhouse.

"I don't understand why they broke into the greenhouse. There are only plants here. I think a child did it. One of them left a toy behind. Some kind of a computer game," the other person said.

"And what did the children steal?" the reporter asked.

"A lot of plants. It's very strange. They came from South America. My grandfather brought them to this country over a hundred years ago," was the answer.

Did you find five things wrong with the story? If you aren't sure what they are, look at the video again.

Focus One

What do we taste/hear/smell/see with?

What's the right word: *tongue*, *ear*, *nose* or *eye*?

What's the right word: *tastes, smells, hears* or *sees?*

5 She______with her eyes.
6 He______with his ears.
7 She______with her nose.
8 She______with her tongue.

1	2	3	4	5	6	7	8

Focus Two

between/behind/in front of

What are the right words: *between*, *behind* or *in front of*?

1 The woman is______the man.
2 He is standing______her.

3 The boy is standing______the two girls. One of them is on his left and the other is on his right.

1	2	3

Focus Three

Don't ______ !

Find the right sentences (a–d) for the pictures (1–4).

a) Don't put it here! Put it over there!
b) Don't make a noise! She's sleeping!
c) Don't watch television! Go to bed!
d) Don't go! I love you!

1	2	3	4

Focus Four

going to do/is doing/has done

Look at the three examples below. Then do the exercise.

What is she going to do?

She's going to eat the sandwich.

What is she doing?

She is eating the sandwich.

What has she done?

She has eaten the sandwich.

Choose the right answer to the questions: **a**) or **b**) ?

1 What is the cat going to do?

a) It has eaten the bird.
b) It is going to eat the bird.

2 What has the cat done?

a) It has eaten the bird.
b) It is going to eat the bird.

1	2

Unit 8

Review

1 Answer these questions about unit 8.

1 What did Inspector Marvin show Orwell?
2 Inspector Marvin asked Orwell some questions. How many of them can you remember?

3 Sabina asked Sline some questions about the drug. What were they?
4 How did Sline answer the questions?

5 Where did Sline, Sabina and Harry go?
6 What did they steal?

2 Now complete these sentences.

1 Marvin showed Orwell .... and asked ....
2 'Have you .... before?' he asked.
3 'Why didn't .... ?' Sabina asked Sline.
4 'There was something I .... You have to use .... ,' Sline told her.
5 Whey they got to Brighton, they .... and ....
6 Harry had a toy in his pocket. It .... and Sline ....

3 Test. Find the right words.

1 Have you ____________ (see/seen/saw) episode 10?
2 The Mepatec civilisation ____________ (comes/has come/came) to an end a long time ago.
3 What did Harry ____________ (leave/left/leaving) behind in the greenhouse?
4 ____________ (Do/Did/Have) you eaten anything today?
5 Please don't ____________ (made/make/making) any noise.
6 I can't understand you because you're speaking ____________ (much/too/very) fast.
7 What's that noise? Where is it coming ____________ (to/from/into)?
8 Orwell thought there were no Telo plants ____________ (of/in/at) Europe.
9 Marvin and Orwell looked ____________ (at/on/to) the photographs.
10 Perhaps some children broke ____________ (in/to/into) the greenhouse.
11 What did they steal ____________ (out/from/of) the greenhouse?
12 They took the man ____________ (at/to/in) the police station.

Unit 9

WE HAVE TO STOP HIM

Preview

1 Can you remember episode 8?

1. Who is the man on the right?
2. Why is he there?
3. The man on the left said, 'It's very strange.' What did he mean?
4. What did someone leave behind?
5. What did someone take away?

2 People say these things in episode 9. What do you think they are talking about?

Example: Have you ever been there?
Perhaps they are talking about a foreign country, or a restaurant somewhere.

1. He's too dangerous. We have to stop him.
2. Would you like milk or sugar in it?
3. There was only one other copy, and that was in the British Library.
4. This time it will work. This time it will be very strong.
5. I'm going to test it.
6. How does it work? I don't know this one.

Look again at 1, 3, 4 and 5. Can you guess who said them?

3 Here are some important words (1–8) from episode 9. Find the connections (a–h).

1 coffee	**a)** buy
2 petrol	**b)** drink
3 bread	**c)** fast
4 cigars	**d)** nose
5 shops	**e)** entrance
6 run	**f)** eat
7 doors	**g)** car
8 smell	**h)** smoke

4 Here are some more things people say. Who do you think says them?

We were behind them. They didn't see us. We put a microphone in their car.

Don't worry. He's not going to do anything. We know where his laboratory is. We know what he's doing there.

Now we can have all the things we've ever wanted. We can start a new life. In another country.

A drink, boss? No thanks, I'm not thirsty. I really don't want one.

101:09
113:36

Watch episode 9. Then do exercises 1 and 2.

Exercise 1

Look at the pictures (1–6). In which pictures did they say these things?

a) He's too dangerous. We have to stop him.
b) Good. So you bought some cigars, then?
c) Is everything all right, boss? Have I done something wrong?
d) This time everything is going to be all right. Nothing can stop me now. Nothing!
e) How much is that?
f) If you press this button, he runs to the left, and if you press the other button, he runs to the right.

1	2	3	4	5	6

Exercise 2

True or false?

1 The two Americans wanted to find out more about Professor Sline's plans.
2 Orwell read the missing page and found out that there were no Telo plants in England.
3 Inspector Marvin got a very important phone call in his office.
4 Orwell wanted to go to a place called Ealing.
5 At first Dr Roberts didn't want to go to Ealing.
6 Sline tested the drug before Harry came back.
7 Sline was very angry because Harry forgot to buy his cigars.
8 Harry didn't want a drink because he wasn't thirsty.

1	2	3	4	5	6	7	8

Now watch this part again. Then do exercises 3 and 4.

101.30
103.57

Exercise 3

What does it mean: **a**) or **b**)?

1 We have to stop him now, before it's too late.

a) It's too late now. We can't stop him.

b) We have to stop him now or it will be too late.

2 Look, I can't waste any more time.

a) I have to do something now because there isn't enough time.

b) I'll wait. I have more time.

1	2

Exercise 4

True or false?

1 Inspector Marvin listened to part of the conversation between Sabina and Sline in the car.

2 George and Alice (the two Americans) said, 'We lost them then. We couldn't get any more.'

3 They said, 'We know who's going to buy the drug from him. And we know what's going to happen then.'

4 They asked, 'Who wants the drug from him? Who's going to buy it? And what's going to happen then?'

5 George and Alice asked questions about Sline, and Inspector Marvin answered them.

1	2	3	4	5

104.00
104.32

Now watch this part again. Then do exercise 5.

Exercise 5

Which word is missing?

a) Are **b)** am **c)** is **d)** Is **e)** Nothing **f)** Nothing **g)** everything **h)** good **i)** right

1	2	3	4	5	6	7	8	9

104:37
107:14

Now watch this part. Then do exercise 6.

Exercise 6

What's wrong with the story? Read it carefully. There is something in it that Orwell didn't say. What is it? And there's something here that Inspector Marvin didn't say. What?

The Lost Secret

Inspector Marvin was sitting in his office behind a big desk when Dr Roberts and Orwell came in to see him.

"Please sit down," he said.

Then he handed them a copy of a page. It was the page from the book about the plants of South America. Orwell took out his glasses and looked at it very carefully.

"It came this morning. There was only one other copy of the book, and that was in the British Library," Marvin said.

Orwell began to read it.

"I didn't know this before," he said.

"The Telo plant used to grow only in one part of South America. But in 1868, after his third visit to South America, Sir Patrick Norton brought back one male and one female Telo plant to England. These were the first and only Telo plants that grew outside South America."

Orwell took off his glasses and looked at Marvin.

"This is why we came here. . . . On the midday news today, we saw . . ." he began, but Marvin stopped him.

"I know. Sline stole the Telo plants from Norton House, near Brighton," he said.

Orwell suddenly stood up. Marvin and Dr Roberts looked at him.

"So you know! Well, what are you going to do about it? He's got the Telo plants. He can make a very dangerous drug with them, much stronger than the one . . ."

Marvin stopped him again.

"I know, Dr Orwell, I know."

"He's going to . . ."

"Don't worry. He's not going to do anything. We know where his laboratory is. We know what he's doing there. And we're going to stop him tomorrow. Or in a few days," Marvin said.

Exercise 7

Then there was a telephone call for Inspector Marvin.
Look at what Marvin said (1–5).
What do you think the other person said: **a**), **b**) or **c**)?

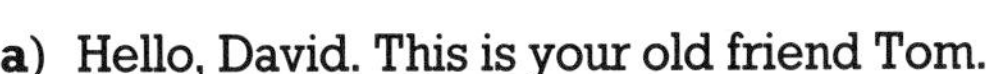

a) Hello, David. This is your old friend Tom.
b) Hello, David. This is your mother.
c) Hello. This is Chief Inspector Andrews.

1 Oh, hello, sir. Good afternoon.

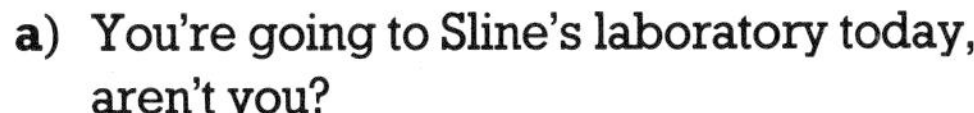

a) You're going to Sline's laboratory today, aren't you?
b) You think Sline is very dangerous, don't you?
c) Are you going to the cinema this evening?

2 Yes, sir, that's right, I am.

a) Are you very busy today?
b) And I understand you've told the Americans about your plans ?
c) When are you going to stop Sline?

3 Yes, sir, I have.

a) Well, I think you should go to Sline's laboratory today.
b) Well, I think you should wait a few days.
c) What are you going to do now?

4 But...but isn't that dangerous? Well, shouldn't we...?

a) I'm sorry, Marvin. But I have my orders.
b) Can you see me now?
c) Are you angry with me?

5 Ah... I see. I think I understand. Very well, sir.

1	2	3	4	5

Exercise 8

Marvin said these things to Orwell later.
But what do they mean: **a**) or **b**)?

1 We can't do anything today.
a) There is nothing we can do today.
b) There are only a few things we can do today.

2 Those are my orders.
a) I'm the boss here!
b) I have to do this.

1	2

107:14
108:52

Now watch this part again. Then do exercises 9 to 12.

Exercise 9

Read this part of the story. Then answer true or false.

The Lost Secret

"Ealing!" Orwell suddenly said. He and Dr Roberts were in her car. She was driving. She didn't understand at first. He said the same name again.

"It's a place. It's a suburb of London," he explained. She already knew that but she still didn't understand why he was talking about Ealing.

1 Ealing is the name of a person.
2 Ealing is the name of a place.
3 Dr Roberts didn't know that Ealing is a suburb of London.
4 A suburb is in the centre of a city.

1	2	3	4

Exercise 10

Find the conversation. Read what Orwell says (1–6). Then put Dr Roberts' answers (a–f) in the right order.

1 Have you ever been there?
2 Do you know it very well?
3 Is there an amusement park there?
4 Yes, an amusement park. Is there an amusement park . . . ?
5 That was the name in the file.
6 The file on Marvin's desk. The file with the photographs. Sline's photograph. Sabina's photograph. It was full of information.

a) What file?
b) Yes, once or twice. Why?
c) You mean you looked . . . ?
d) No, not very well, but . . .
e) Amusement park?
f) What are you talking about? Why are you asking?

1	2	3	4	5	6

Exercise 11

Now read this part. Then find the right answer: **a**) or **b**)?

The Lost Secret

"That's where his laboratory is – in some kind of amusement park," he told her.

Dr Roberts didn't say anything. He looked at her.

"Well?"

She still didn't say anything.

"Let's go there now!" he said.

"No! We can't! Remember what Inspector Marvin said!" she answered.

"But Sline can make the drug now. And this time it'll work!"

She looked out of the window. She was thinking.

"I know. But Inspector Marvin said we have to wait," she said.

"But we have to stop him!"

She didn't want to talk about it any more. He looked at her.

"Perhaps she's angry," he thought.

"We have to find a garage. We have to get some petrol," she said suddenly.

"Why now?" he asked.

"There isn't enough petrol to get there."

"Where?" he asked.

"Ealing!" she answered. He was surprised. Then he laughed. Dr Roberts laughed too.

1 An amusement park is a park with a lot of . . .
a) grass and trees.
b) games and things like that.

2 Dr Roberts didn't say anything because she didn't . . .
a) understand Orwell.
b) want to go to Ealing.

3 Was Dr Roberts really angry?
a) Yes.
b) No.

4 Petrol is something you . . .
a) put in your car to make it go.
b) put in your mouth and eat.

5 What did Dr Roberts want to get at a garage?
a) some information
b) some petrol

6 Did she and Orwell go to Ealing?
a) Yes.
b) No.

1	2	3	4	5	6

Exercise 12

Find the best explanation: **a**), **b**) or **c**)?

1 suburb
a) the centre of a town
b) somewhere outside the centre of a town
c) somewhere where you buy petrol

2 You are surprised when . . .
a) you feel angry.
b) you didn't know something was going to happen.
c) you know something that somebody else doesn't know.

3 place
a) a building
b) a city or town
c) where something is – a room or building or town or city etc

4 file
a) something you can put papers and other information in
b) a kind of table or chair
c) an office

1	2	3	4

108:58
110:47

Now watch this part again. Then do exercises 13 and 14.

Exercise 13

Which word is missing: **a**), **b**) or **c**)?

The smell of fresh bread — __2__ you remember? When we made the drug before, the smell was the __3__ – fresh bread – only this is __4__ stronger. Oh, I'm sorry, I forgot! You can't smell __5__, can you?

1 a) been
b) be
c) is

2 a) doesn't
b) didn't
c) don't

3 a) same
b) like
c) as

4 a) much
b) many
c) very

5 a) nothing
b) something
c) anything

6 a) much
b) many
c) very

7 a) are
b) is
c) can

8 a) going
b) gone
c) go

9 a) What
b) How
c) Who

10 a) go
b) gone
c) goes

1	2	3	4	5	6	7	8	9	10

Exercise 14

What happened next? Did they say these things? Answer yes or no.

1 Now I can have all the things I've ever wanted. I can start a new life.
2 Have you ever been to Brazil?
3 A big country.
4 I haven't forgotten that, Sabina.
5 Yes, I live there.
6 We still have to test this drug.
7 I think there's enough for the test. Yes, there's more than enough. It's ready!

1	2	3	4	5	6	7

110:48
111:50

Watch this part again. Read the cartoon strip. Then do exercises 15 and 16.

Exercise 15

Are the sentences (1–6) below true or false?

Well, you press this button, and a little man comes up in the corner. He runs to the left and he runs to the right. Do you see? If you press this button, he runs to the left, and if you press the other button, he runs to the right.

1 All the computer games are £4.50.
2 Some of them are cheaper than others.
3 The price of the game Harry is looking at is £12.99.
4 There is only one button.
5 The little man can run to the right or to the left.
6 Harry isn't going to buy the game.

1	2	3	4	5	6

Exercise 16

Which sentence goes with each cartoon: **a)** or **b)**?

1 The man is standing . . .
a) in the corner of the street.
b) at the corner of the street.

2 The television is . . .
a) at the corner of the room.
b) in the corner of the room.

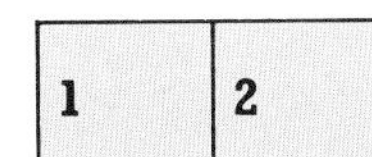

1	2

111:51
113:36

Watch this part again. Then do exercises 17, 18 and 19.

Exercise 17

There are three things wrong with the story. What are they?

The Lost Secret

"Is this the centre of Ealing?" Orwell asked.

"I think so. But where can I park the car?" Dr Roberts answered. Orwell wasn't really listening. He was looking out of the window. He could remember some doors. They were green and they were the doors of a building near the centre of Ealing. He knew that Sline's laboratory was in that building.

"Look!" he suddenly shouted. "There's Harry, Sline's driver!"

Dr Roberts saw him for a moment. Then, suddenly, he wasn't there.

"But where's he gone?" she asked. She stopped the car. "We have to find him. We have to find him!" she shouted. She jumped out of the car. Orwell jumped out too and ran after her.

Exercise 18

Now put these parts of the story in the correct order.

a) "Good. So you bought some cigars, then?" Sline asked him.

"Cigars, boss?" Harry was worried again.

"Yes, the cigars. Did you buy them?" Sline said. He was still smiling, but Harry was still worried.

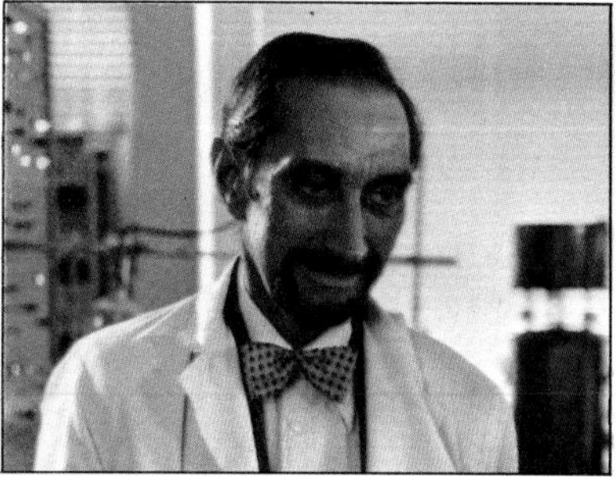

b) When Harry came into the laboratory, Sline turned around.

"Ah, there you are. Where have you been?" he said. He laughed. Harry was worried. His boss didn't laugh very often.

"Oh, I'm sorry, boss. Am I late? Have I done something wrong?"

Sline smiled.

c) She smiled, too. But Harry wasn't thirsty. He didn't want a drink, and told Sline so. But the professor only smiled again.

"But you will like this drink, Harry. You really will," he said.

d) "No, no, Harry. Everything's just fine," he told him. Harry felt better. He tried to smile too.

"I got all the things you wanted, boss," he said.

e) "No, no, it doesn't matter, Harry. There are more important things in life than cigars," he said. He looked at Sabina.
"Get Harry a drink," he told her.

f) Harry knew something was wrong. This time he was sure that Sline was angry. But he couldn't understand why he was smiling.
"I'm sorry, boss. I forgot your cigars. I'll go back and get them," he said. He began to get up, but Sline stopped him.

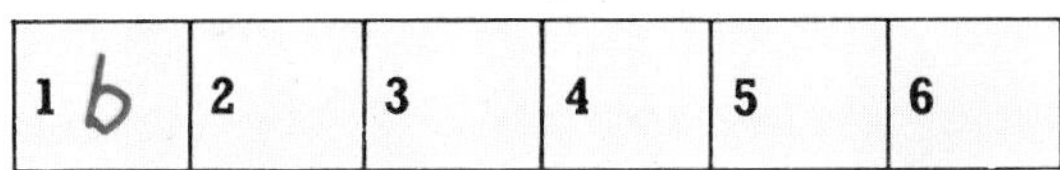

1 b	2	3	4	5	6

Exercise 19

What's the difference between *laugh* and *smile*?
Who is laughing? The man or the woman? Which one is only smiling?

Exercise 20

Look at these examples of questions and short answers. Now fill in the missing words.

Is this the centre of Ealing?
– Yes, it is./No, it isn't.
Are you from Ealing?
– Yes, I am./No, I'm not.
Do you speak English?
– Yes, I do./No, I don't.

Can you see Harry?
– Yes, I can./No, I can't.
Did she sleep well last night?
– Yes, she did./No, she didn't.
Have you been to Brazil?
Yes, I have./No, I haven't.

Have they ever seen Rio?
– Yes, they have./No, they haven't.
Is he a teacher?
– Yes, he is./No, he isn't.
Have we been here before?
– Yes, we have./No, we haven't.

Which word is missing from these answers?

1 Is Orwell an archeologist?
Yes, he ______.
2 Is Harry a professor?
No, he ______.
3 Has Sabina ever been to Brazil?
Yes, she ______.
4 Has Sline ever been to Brazil?
No, he ______.

1	2	3	4

Now write short answers to these questions.

5 Have you ever been to Brazil? ______.
6 Are you from Brazil? ______.
7 Can you speak Portuguese? ______.
8 Did you sleep well last night? ______.

5	6	7	8

Focus One

something/nothing/anything/everything

Find the missing word. Is it *something, nothing, anything* or *everything*?

There's ___1___ in the glass. It's empty.

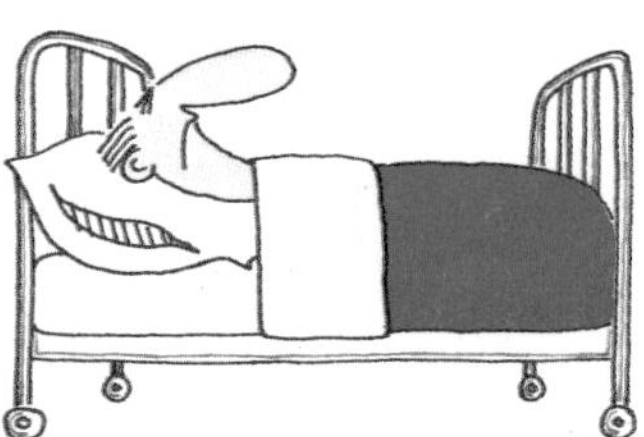

Paul is in hospital. He's very ill. He can't eat. He can't drink. He can't walk. He needs a lot of help. He can't do ___2___ .

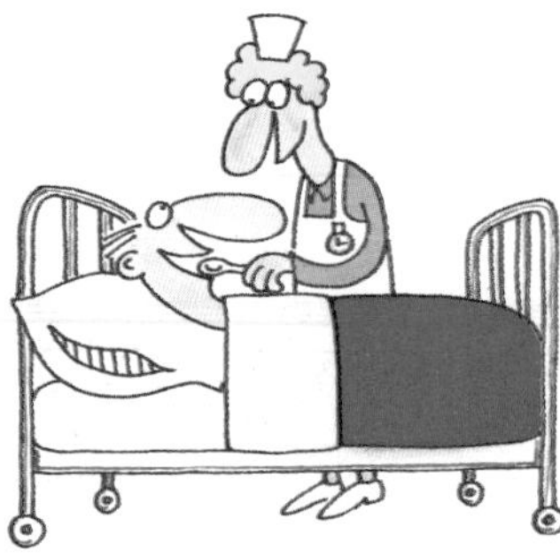

Jane works in the hospital. She takes care of Paul. He needs a lot of help, so she has to do ___3___ for him.

There's ___4___ in his pocket. He can't remember what it is, but he knows it's there.

1	2	3	4

Focus Two

I/He/She used to ______ .

Find the right sentence for each picture.

1

2

3

4

a) I used to ride a bicycle when I was a boy. Now I'm too old.
b) She used to watch a lot of television when she was a girl. Now she reads a lot.
c) He used to have a lot of hair when he was a boy. Now he hasn't got any.
d) She used to play with toys when she was a girl. Now she sells them.

1	2	3	4

Focus Three

If  .

If you press this button, the television goes on.

If you eat too much, you get fat.

If you turn the key, the car starts.

What's the right answer: **a**) or **b**)?

1 If you take the memory drug . . .
a) you forget things.
b) you remember things.

2 If you don't drink . . .
a) you get hungry.
b) you get thirsty.

1	2

Focus Four

been/gone

What does it mean: **a**) or **b**)?

1 She's gone to London.
a) She's in London now.
b) She was in London, but she's here now.

2 He's been to hospital.
a) He's in the hospital now.
b) He was in the hospital, but he's here now.

1	2

Unit 9

Review

1 These things happened in episode 9 (a–j). Put them in the right order (1–10).

a) Inspector Marvin had a phone call.
b) They saw Harry from the car.
c) 'We have to stop him,' Inspector Marvin told Alice and George.
d) Sline smiled at Harry. 'Where have you been?' he asked.
e) 'We can't do anything today. We have to wait,' he told Orwell.
f) Harry bought a computer game in a shop.
g) 'He's got the Telo plants,' Orwell told Marvin.
h) 'Get Harry a drink,' he told Sabina.
i) 'Ealing! That's where his laboratory is. Let's go there now!' Orwell said to Dr Roberts.
j) Orwell and Dr Roberts saw Inspector Marvin in his office.

2 Here is a picture from episode 10. Can you answer the questions?

1 Who are they?
2 What do you think they can see?
3 Where are they?

3 Test. Find the right words.

1 I ____________ (has/have/should) to buy some things at the shop.
2 Have you ever been to America?
—Yes, I ____________ (have been/were/was) there in 1985.
3 When ____________ (did you see/have you seen/you saw) that film?
4 When I was very young I ____________ (use to play/used to play/have played) football, but I don't any more.
5 This bottle's empty. There's ____________ (anything/something/nothing) in it.
6 I'm not hungry. I don't want ____________ (anything/something/nothing) to eat.
7 We don't have enough petrol. We ____________ (have/would/should) stop at a garage.
8 ____________ (Is/Is it/Is there) a garage near here?
9 I need some petrol.
—I'm sorry. We haven't got ____________ (it/some/any).
10 She's seen that film before, ____________ (doesn't/isn't/hasn't) she?

Unit 10

THE RED DOORS

Preview

1 Here is a picture from episode 10. Can you answer the questions?

1. Who do you think this is?
2. What do you think is happening?
3. Who are the drinks for?
4. What is in them?
5. What do you think will happen next?

2 Now look at these pictures. How do you think these people feel? Why?

3 Here are some important words (1–6) from episode 10. Find the connections (a–f).

1 trousers	**a)** cook
2 kitchen	**b)** gun
3 shoot	**c)** apples
4 fruit	**d)** memory
5 cheers	**e)** wear
6 forget	**f)** drink

4 Here are some things people say in episode 10. Who do you think says them? Who are they speaking to? Where are they?

How did they find the laboratory? How did they know where to go?

So you've come to see us again. Isn't that nice, Harry?

You know this man, don't you? You remember his name.

Don't worry. We're here to help you.

113:48
126:04

Watch episode 10. Then do exercises 1 and 2.

Exercise 1

Match the pictures (1–6) with the sentences (a–f).

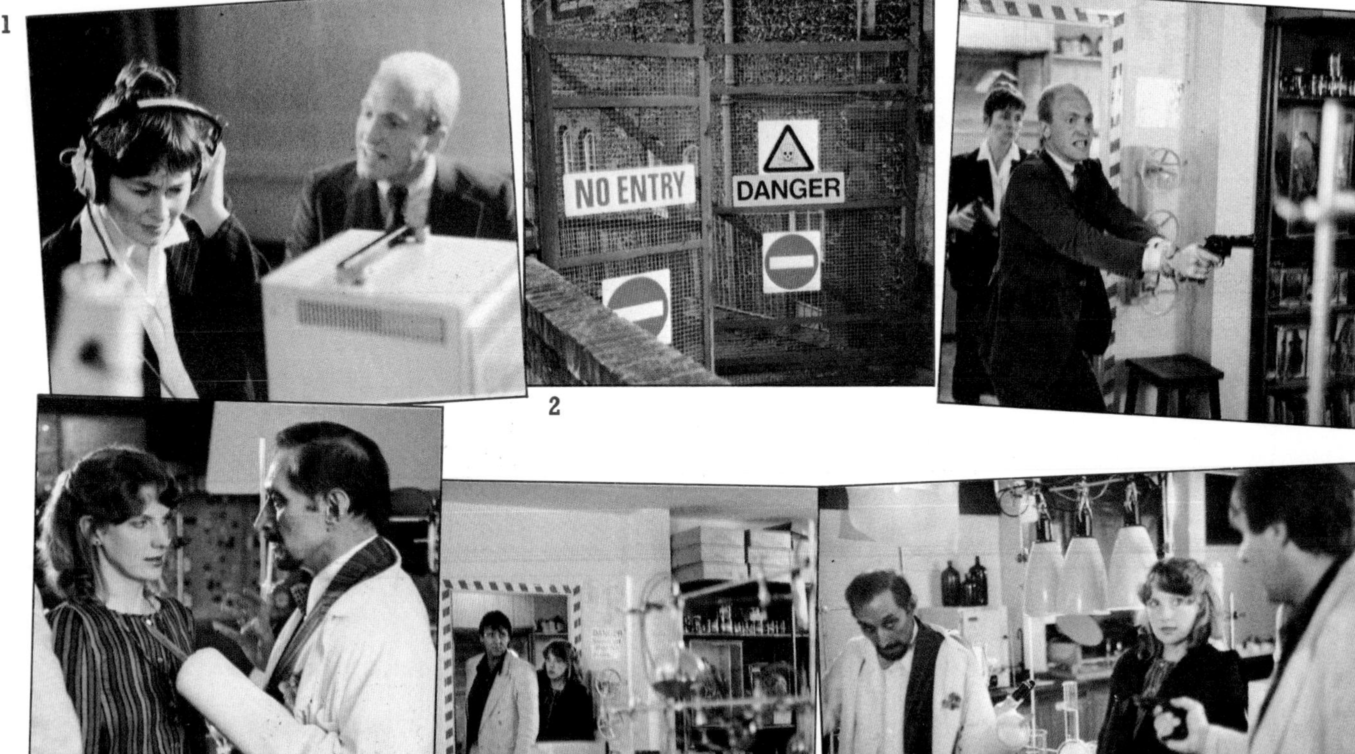

1 2 4 5 6

a) They saw two gates. There were signs on them.
b) 'Shh! I'm listening,' she told him.
c) They looked into the laboratory. 'It's empty. There's nobody here,' she said.
d) 'So you've come to see us again. Isn't that nice, Harry? But who is your friend?' he asked.
e) They were very surprised. 'What is this? What's happened here?' one of them asked.
f) He had the gun in his hand. 'Don't shoot him,' she said.

1	2	3	4	5	6

Exercise 2

True or false?

1 Sabina gave Harry a drink, but he never drank it.
2 She gave Sline a drink too.
3 The memory drug was in only one of the drinks.
4 When Orwell and Dr Roberts went into the laboratory, they thought it was empty.
5 When Inspector Marvin and the police came, Sabina was still in the laboratory.
6 When the police came, Professor Sline wasn't a dangerous man any more.

1	2	3	4	5	6

114:08
116:43

Watch this part again. Then do exercises 3 and 4.

Exercise 3

Read the story. Can you find what is wrong with it?

The Lost Secret

"What kind of drink is it, boss?" Harry asked.

"It's a fruit drink. It's in the kitchen," Sabina told him. Then she smiled at him. But it was a very strange smile. She didn't like Harry. In fact, she hated him. But she tried not to show it.

"I'll get it for you," she said, and went into the kitchen quickly.

Nobody could see her there. First she filled three glasses with the fruit drink. She put the memory drug in two of them and went back to the laboratory.

"Here you are," she said, and gave Harry one of the glasses.

"And here's one for you," she said to Sline, and gave him the other drink with the memory drug in it. She put his glass on the table and put her glass next to it. Then she turned away.

Sline looked at the two glasses.

"Perhaps she has put some memory drug in this drink, too," he thought. Then he did something with the two glasses. Sabina couldn't see him.

Sline looked at Harry and smiled again.

"I hope you like it. I'm sure you will. Come on, Harry. Drink up! Cheers!" he said. He looked at Sabina, too.

"What about you?" he asked her.

She smiled.

"Yes. To our new life! And to the memory drug!" she answered. She didn't know that her drink had the memory drug in it, too.

Exercise 4

What is the right answer: **a**), **b**) or **c**)?

1 What does 'hate' mean?
a) to like
b) not to like at all
c) to watch carefully

2 What did Sline mean when he said, 'Drink up!' to Harry?
a) drink all of it
b) drink some of it
c) drink very little

3 And what did he mean when he said, 'What about you, Sabina?'
a) What is that on you?
b) What did you say?
c) Why aren't you drinking?

4 A kitchen is a place where . . .
a) you sleep.
b) you make things to eat.
c) you put your car.

1	2	3	4

116:43
120:05

Now watch this part again. Then do exercises 5 to 9.

Exercise 5

What is the right word: **a**), **b**) or **c**)?

1 a) gone
b) went
c) goes

2 a) saw
b) seen
c) see

3 a) are
b) is
c) be

4 a) happen
b) happens
c) happening

5 a) see
b) look
c) watch

6 a) going
b) gone
c) went

7 a) going
b) gone
c) go

8 a) first
b) then
c) last

9 a) making
b) made
c) make

10 a) drink
b) drinking
c) drunk

1	2	3	4	5	6	7	8	9	10

Exercise 6

Read the six parts of the story (a–f).
Put them in the right order (1–6).

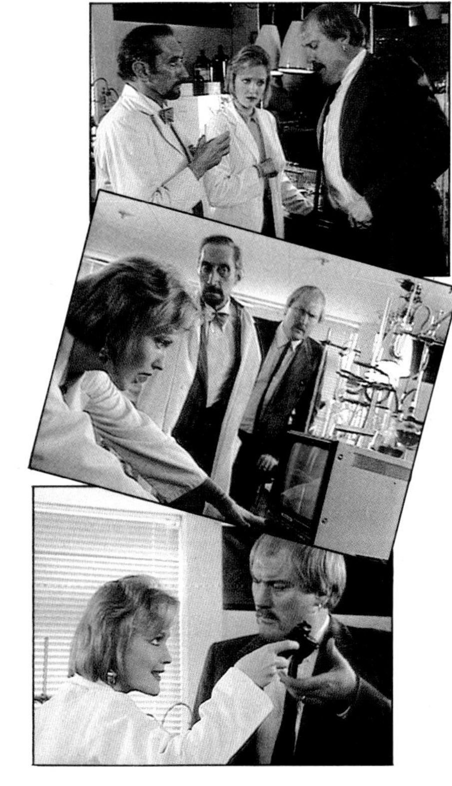

a) "They're too tight. I think I'll have to buy some new ones," Harry said. Sline heard him but didn't really understand.
"Yes. Yes. New what? What did you say?" he asked.
"Trousers," Harry said again.

b) Sabina went to the television and looked. She saw Orwell with Dr Roberts.
"It's Orwell . . . with a woman. They're outside the door!" she said.

c) "What's wrong, Harry?" Sline asked.
"It's nothing, boss. Nothing. Just my trousers," Harry answered.

d) Suddenly Sline heard a noise.
"Did you hear it? Is there someone outside? Find out!" he said to Sabina.

e) "You know what to do! Take this!" Sabina said to Harry, and gave him a gun.

f) Sline began to feel very strange. He looked at Harry and asked, "Your trousers? What's wrong with your trousers?"

1	2	3	4	5	6

Exercise 7

What does it mean: **a)** or **b)**?

1 What's the drink made of?
a) Where did you buy it?
b) What is in it?

2 His trousers are too tight.
a) They are too small.
b) They are too big.

1	2

Exercise 8

Match the words and the pictures.

a) an orange
b) an apple
c) some grapes

1	2	3

Exercise 9

Look at the woman and find her . . .

a) coat
b) hat
✓ **c)** boots
d) dress
e) handbag

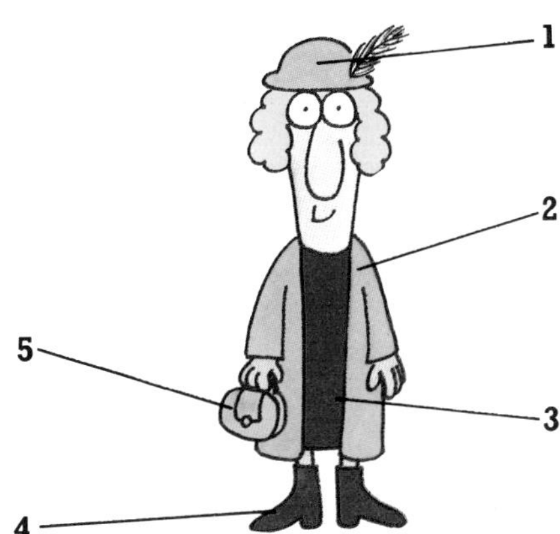

120:10
126:04

Now watch this part again. Then do exercises 10 to 14.

Exercise 10

What is the right word: **a**), **b**) or **c**)?

1 a) somebody
b) anybody
c) nobody

2 a) somewhere
b) anywhere
c) nowhere

3 a) coming
b) came
c) come

4 a) where
b) who
c) what

5 a) something
b) anything
c) everything

6 a) haven't
b) aren't
c) didn't

7 a) been
b) being
c) was

8 a) can't
b) don't
c) aren't

9 a) given
b) gives
c) gave

10 a) know
b) knows
c) knew

1	2	3	4	5	6	7	8	9	10

Exercise 11

Read this. Then answer the questions.

The Lost Secret

She was an American, and her name was Alice. She was in a room near Sline's laboratory and she was listening to two people. One of them was a man and the other was a woman.

"Oh, come now, Professor, you know who he is. You know that. Think!" one of them said.

"Yes, that's right. I've seen him before. But have I seen you before?" the other answered.

There was another American in the room. He was talking to someone on the telephone.

"Are you sure? 'Bye," the man said, and put the phone down. He turned to the woman.

"They say he's coming here," he told her.

She was still listening to the two people.

"What?"

"They say he . . ." he began again, but the woman stopped him.

"Shh! I'm listening," she said. She looked worried, very worried. She took off the headphones and looked at him.

"Marvin is coming here. He left almost an hour ago," the man said slowly and carefully.

"We can't wait for him. We have to get in there!" the woman answered.

She got up. So did the man. They left the room quickly. Both of them had guns.

What is the right answer: **a**), **b**) or **c**)?

1 The woman could hear two people because
a) two people were talking to her.
b) she was listening through some headphones.
c) there was something wrong with her head.

2 Who said, 'Oh, come now, Professor, you know who he is'?
a) Dr Roberts
b) Sabina
c) a woman on the telephone

3 Who said, 'Yes, that's right. I've seen him before'?
a) the other American
b) Orwell
c) Sline

4 Where was the other American?
a) in the laboratory
b) in another room
c) in the room with Alice

5 Who do you think he was talking to on the telephone?
a) Alice
b) Inspector Marvin
c) someone who works with Marvin

6 Who was the American talking about when he said, 'They say *he's* coming here'?
a) Sline
b) Inspector Marvin
c) their boss

7 What did Alice mean when she said, 'We have to get in there'?
a) We have to bring them here.
b) We have to get an answer to this question.
c) We have to go to the laboratory.

8 What does the word 'them' mean in 'Both of them had guns'?
a) Harry and Sline
b) Dr Roberts and Orwell
c) the two Americans, Alice and George

1	2	3	4	5	6	7	8

Exercise 12

Where should these words go?

a) happened **b)** happens **c)** in **d)** about **e)** short **f)** long **g)** quickly **h)** slowly

1	2	3	4	5	6	7	8

Now read this.

The Lost Secret

There was something wrong with Sline. He didn't know what it was. But when Dr Roberts said, "Then you forget everything!" something happened to him. Suddenly he understood the terrible truth. The drug was beginning to destroy his memory.

The drug was working on Harry too. He was looking at the gun in his hand. He couldn't understand why it was there. Suddenly Orwell took it from him. Harry didn't move. He just stood there.

"No, no, no. No!" Sline shouted. He turned to Orwell. He wanted to kill him. He began to come nearer and nearer with the knife. Orwell moved back.

Dr Roberts looked at the gun in his hand and shouted, "Don't shoot him."

Sline came nearer. Orwell moved back again. Sline suddenly ran at him with the knife. Orwell quickly moved to the left. He was too fast for Sline. The professor ran into the door. His knife went into the door too.

Orwell looked at the gun in his hand. He hated guns. He quickly put it on the table.

"Where's Sabina?" he asked Dr Roberts.

"I think she's gone."

"Was she here when we came in?"

"I don't know, but someone gave them the memory drug," she answered, and looked at Harry and Sline. Then she asked, "Who do you think that was?"

Suddenly the door opened. A man and a woman came in with guns in their hands.

Exercise 13

True or false?

1 Sline remembered Orwell's name when he saw Dr Roberts with him.
2 Orwell wanted to take the gun from Harry, but Harry stopped him.
3 Dr Roberts wanted to shoot Sline.
4 The professor ran out of the laboratory and into the street.
5 Dr Roberts didn't think that Sabina gave Sline and Harry the memory drug.
6 The man and the woman with guns were the two Americans.

1	2	3	4	5	6

Exercise 14

Which word is missing?

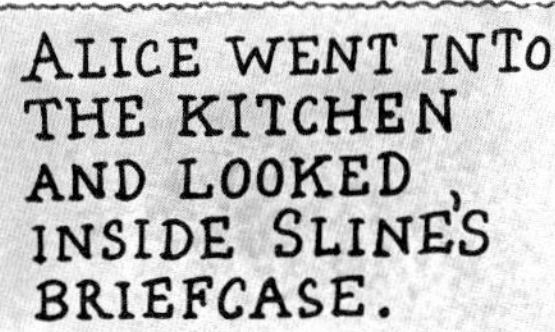

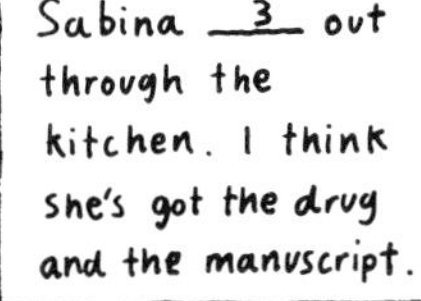

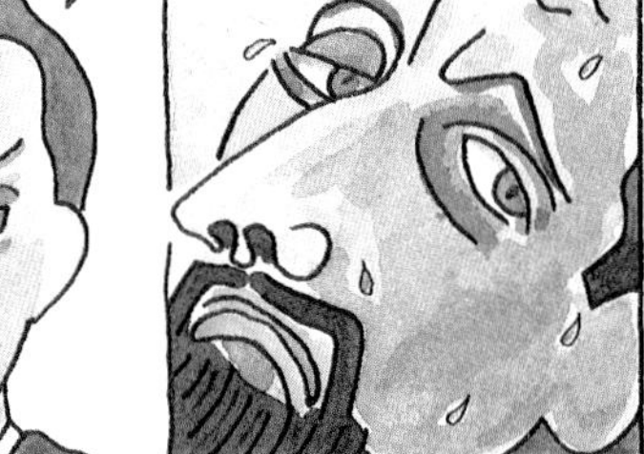

1	a) happen	2	a) gave	3	a) went	4	a) all	5	a) found
	b) happens		b) given		b) goes		b) every		b) find
	c) happened		c) giving		c) gone		c) both		c) finding

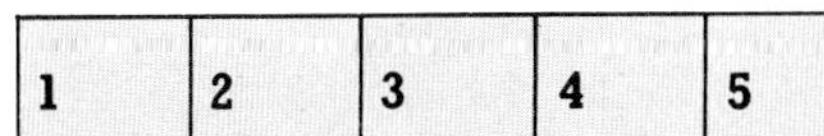

1	2	3	4	5

Exercise 15

What did Inspector Marvin say then?

a) You have been a very dangerous man.
b) You will be a very dangerous man.
c) You were a very dangerous man.

Focus One

I/You haven't ______ yet. He/She hasn't ______ yet.

Find the right sentence for each picture.

a) No, he hasn't. He's late.
b) I don't know. I haven't seen it yet. I'm just going in.
c) No, you can't. You haven't finished your work yet.
d) No, she doesn't. I haven't told her yet.

1	2	3	4

Focus Two

both/all/some

Look at these examples.

Now find the missing word. Is it *both, all* or *some*?

__1__ of her parents are dead.

He can't make a sandwich because someone has eaten __2__ the bread.

__3__ people don't like aeroplanes.

Focus Three

slowly/quickly/carefully/well

Find the right sentence for each picture.

a) Please come quickly, doctor. My mother is very ill.
b) She drives well. She's a good driver.
c) Eat slowly! You're not late for school.
d) He drives badly. He's a bad driver.
e) Drink it carefully! It's very hot!

1	2	3	4	5

Focus Four

has/is

The train is coming.

The train has arrived.

Is the *'s* in these sentences *is* or *has*?

1 She's coming tomorrow.
2 What's he done now?
3 What's he doing now?
4 She's been here for three hours.
5 He's broken the bottle.
6 He's breaking the bottle.
7 Where's he going?
8 Where's she gone?
9 She's driving too fast.
10 He's gone to London.

1	2	3	4	5
6	7	8	9	10

Unit 10

Review

1 These things (a–l) happened in episode 10. First put them in the right order (1–12). Then use them to write a summary in the past tense.

a) George and Alice come into the laboratory with guns in their hands.
b) When Orwell and Dr Roberts go into the laboratory, they can't see anyone.
c) Sline changes his glass and Sabina's. They all drink.
d) At the same time, Sabina is in the kitchen. She is putting things in a bag.
e) Marvin comes in and sees Sline on the floor.
f) Sline takes off his glove. There is a knife there, not a hand.
g) She gives the drink to Sline and Harry in the laboratory.
h) Suddenly Sline and Harry are behind them. Harry has a gun.
i) Alice goes into the kitchen. Sabina isn't there.
j) The drug is beginning to work when Sline hears a strange noise. Orwell and Dr Roberts are outside!
k) In the kitchen, Sabina puts the memory drug in two glasses of fruit juice.
l) Orwell takes the gun from Harry's hand. Then Sline runs at him with the knife.

2 Look at these pictures from episode 11. What do you think?

1 Where did Orwell go?
2 What did he find?
3 Why was it important?
4 What did he do with it?

3 Test. Find the right words.

1 Sline knows he ____________ (have/has) seen Orwell before.
2 I know I have ____________ (meet/met) you before, but I can't remember where.
3 Did Sline ____________ (meet/met) Orwell at Alfredo's?
4 ____________ (Has/Did) Sabina put the drug in his drink a minute ago?
5 Harry isn't a ____________ (good/well) driver.
6 He doesn't drive very ____________ (good/well).
7 In fact, he drives very ____________ (bad/badly).
8 He is a ____________ (dangerous/dangerously) driver.

Unit 11

THE END

Preview

1 What happened in episode 10?

1 Do you think Dr Roberts was very worried when she saw Sline?
2 Where was Sabina when this happened?
3 Where was the drug?
4 What happened after this?

2 Here are some things that happen in episode 11. Study them and then answer the questions.

1 She put the black bag down for a second, and tried to find the keys for the car. But they weren't there.
2 'Take your hands off me!' she shouted.
3 When she turned around, she saw a young woman in a dark suit and a man with short blond hair. She didn't know them.
'Who are you? What do you want?' she said.
4 Two years later, a woman was in a bookshop. There were a lot of copies of a book there called *Lost Memories.* Suddenly she heard a man's voice.
'Have you written any other books?' the man asked.
She couldn't see the man's face because he was behind her, but she was sure she knew that voice.

What do you think?

1 Who was the woman who couldn't find her keys?
2 Who did she shout at?
3 What did the woman and the man want? Who were they?
4 Who was the woman in the bookshop? Who was the man?

3 Here are some things people say in episode 11. Who or what do you think they are talking about?

You gave me the idea for the book.

It was a danger to the world! Think what could happen if it got into the wrong hands.

He's in prison. A special kind of prison.

They're dead. And so is their secret.

126:17
137:16

Watch episode 11. Then do exercises 1 and 2.

Exercise 1

Which sentence goes with each picture?

1 2 4 5 6

a) You're coming with us!
b) I found it inside the mountain where they made the drug.
c) What do people put in these bags? This one is really heavy.
d) You've taken it! Give it back to me!
e) I've already read it. It's very interesting.
f) You know, there's one thing I'd like to ask you.

1	2	3	4	5	6

Exercise 2

True or false?

1 Sabina dropped her car keys and never found them again.
2 She tried to get the black bag. But the two men stopped her.
3 The two Americans wanted to help Sabina when they saw her.
4 Orwell met Dr Roberts again in a bookshop a few days later.
5 He brought the memory cup back from South America with him.
6 Harry spends a lot of time in prison reading books.

1	2	3	4	5	6

126:37
128:55

Now watch this part again. Then do exercises 3 and 4.

Exercise 3

What's the right word: **a**), **b**) or **c**)?

1 **a**) than
b) as
c) like

2 **a**) Don't
b) No
c) Not

3 **a**) yours
b) your
c) you

4 **a**) forgotten
b) fallen
c) dropped

5 **a**) This
b) Those
c) These

6 **a**) were
b) was
c) are

7 **a**) happens
b) happened
c) happen

8 **a**) fall
b) fell
c) fallen

9 **a**) keep
b) kept
c) keeping

10 **a**) on
b) at
c) in

1	2	3	4	5	6	7	8	9	10

Exercise 4

What's the right word: **a**), **b**) or **c**)?

1	**2**	**3**	**4**	**5**	**6**	**7**
a) do	**a**) me	**a**) do	**a**) look	**a**) Don't	**a**) took	**a**) have
b) done	**b**) mine	**b**) done	**b**) looks	**b**) No	**b**) take	**b**) has
c) doing	**c**) my	**c**) doing	**c**) looked	**c**) Not	**c**) taken	**c**) having

1	2	3	4	5	6	7

128:56
137:16

Now watch this part again. Then do exercises 5 and 6.

Read this part of the story.

The Lost Secret

It was two years later. Dr Roberts was in a bookshop in Winchester. She was signing copies of her new book, *Lost Memories*. A woman came up to her with a copy of the book.

"Would you sign this, please?" she asked. "I've already read it. It's very interesting."

"I'm glad you enjoyed it," she answered. Then she heard a man's voice behind her.

"Have you written any other books?" he asked.

Dr Roberts heard the man's question, but couldn't see him.

"No, I haven't," she said, and turned around.

"Dr Orwell!" she said. She was very surprised and happy to see him. "How nice to see you! It's been a long time."

"Yes, a long time," Orwell answered. "About two years." He looked happy to see her too.

"You look very well," Dr Roberts said to him.

"Yes, I'm much better, thanks to you," Orwell answered. He smiled.

"Ah, look, it's a nice evening. Have you got time for a walk?" he asked.

Dr Roberts thought for a moment and said, "Well, yes, but I have to be back at the clinic in an hour or so."

Dr Orwell looked pleased. "Well, why don't we walk along the river?" he said. "I'd like to talk to you."

"That would be nice," Dr Roberts answered. They both walked to the door and left the shop. They walked along the river. There were clouds in the sky, but the sun was still shining.

"How are things?" Dr Roberts asked.

Exercise 5

True or false?

1 Dr Roberts saw Orwell before he spoke to her.
2 Dr Roberts had to go back to the clinic later that evening.
3 She didn't want to go for a walk because she was very busy.
4 It was a nice evening, but there were some clouds in the sky.

1	2	3	4

Exercise 6

What does it mean: **a**) or **b**)?

1 The woman enjoyed the book.
a) She liked it.
b) She didn't like it.

2 in an hour or so
a) in an hour or two or three
b) in an hour or a little later

3 How are things?
a) How are you?
b) What have you been doing?

1	2	3

Exercise 7

Find the conversation. Read what Orwell says (1–5). Then put what Dr Roberts says in the right order.

1 Well, I've been back in Winchester for a week.
2 Yes, I went back to South America. I was there for a year. What about you?
3 Yes, *Lost Memories*. Very interesting.
4 Not yet, but I'm going to.
5 Am I in your book?

a) It's about people who lose their memories.
b) Well, as you know, I've written a book.
c) No, you're not, but you gave me the idea for the book.
d) You've been away again?
e) Have you read it yet?

1 d	2	3	4	5

Exercise 8

Now read the second part of the story and find the missing words below.

The Lost Secret

"Memories. Do you __1__ that?" Dr Roberts asked. She stopped and looked at a bridge over the river. Orwell looked at it and smiled.

"Of course. I jumped from that bridge, didn't I?"

Dr Roberts smiled too. They __2__ along the river a little more. Orwell began to ask questions. Dr Roberts told him __3__ Inspector Marvin.

"He doesn't live in Winchester any more. He's been in London since last year. He's got a much __4__ job now," she said.

"You mean he isn't a policeman any more?" Orwell asked.

Dr Roberts smiled again. "No, he's still a policeman, but he's a Chief Inspector now."

Orwell looked at her. "You know, there's one thing I'd like to __5__ you. When you and I broke into Sline's laboratory . . ." He stopped for a moment and then went on. "Sabina gave Sline the memory drug . . ."

"Yes, I knew there was something wrong with him as soon as I saw him," Dr Roberts __6__.

"Yes, but how?" Orwell wanted to know. "I mean, it happened before we broke in."

"The smell," she answered.

At first Orwell didn't understand what she was talking about. Dr Roberts explained what she __7__. There was the smell of fresh bread in the laboratory. She knew that the drug smelt like fresh bread.

The Lost Secret

"I think you told me. Or perhaps I __8__ it in the book we got from the library. And that's what Sline smelt of – fresh bread!"

"Well, why didn't Sline smell it too?" Orwell asked.

Dr Roberts explained about Professor Sline's accident. "He __9__ to work in the United States, for the government there. He worked in some kind of laboratory. And he had a very bad __10__ there. A very bad fire. Don't you remember his hand? It was very badly burnt. He was in hospital for a long time. And perhaps . . . oh, I don't know, but perhaps that's why he couldn't smell," she said.

Orwell looked up at the sky. The sun was still shining a little but the __11__ were getting thicker and greyer. He thought of the bright sun and the very blue sky in South America. And he remembered his last visit to South America. But he didn't want to tell Dr Roberts about that. Not yet.

"Where is he now?" he asked.

"Sline? He's in prison. A special __12__ of prison."

Then he asked about the man who used to work with Sline. At first he couldn't remember his name.

"Harry? He's in the __13__ prison. You know, it's funny. They say Harry's happy in prison. He spends a lot of time in the prison library. He reads a lot. All kinds of books," she __14__ him.

Orwell looked at her. He couldn't believe it.

"Harry? __15__ books? Impossible!" he said.

a) meant
b) better
c) accident
d) Reading
e) remember
f) kind
g) walked
h) used
i) about
j) read
k) same
l) ask
m) told
n) clouds
o) answered

1	2	3	4	5	6	7	8	9	10

11	12	13	14	15

Exercise 9

Now read this part of the story. Then answer the questions about it.

The Lost Secret

The Lost Secret

Then Orwell asked Dr Roberts about Sabina.

"They took her to America," she answered.

"They?" Orwell asked. "Who?"

She told him she wasn't sure who they were. But she thought they were something to do with the American government. She smiled and thought for a moment. "But what about you?" she asked him.

"Me?" he answered. "I've already told you. I went back to South America, back to where the Mepatecs used to live."

"Did you find anything interesting?" she asked.

He looked at her carefully and said, "Yes, I did. I found something very interesting."

"Yes. Go on! What was it?" she asked quickly.

"Do you know about the memory cup?" Orwell asked.

"The memory cup! Yes, you told me about it. Don't you remember?"

"Did I?" he answered. He couldn't remember.

"You told me that the secret of the Mepatecs was on the cup. But you weren't sure that it was a real cup. You said perhaps it was just a story."

"And now I know it wasn't a story," Orwell said. "There really was a memory cup. I know because I found it!"

"Where?" Dr Roberts asked.

"Inside the mountain where they made the drug," he answered. Then he began to tell Dr Roberts his story. He told her about the mountain and how he went inside it. "When I saw the cup," he explained, "I knew that it really was the memory cup. All the secrets of the Mepatecs were on the cup. It explained everything."

"What did it explain?" Dr Roberts asked him.

"Everything! The lost secret of the Mepatecs. How they made the drug, how they used it, how it destroyed their memories. I found out things only Sline knew – Sline and a few people a thousand years ago." Orwell thought for a moment. "It was all there . . . in my hands . . . and I held it in my hands."

"What happened then?" Dr Roberts asked. "What did you do then?"

Orwell looked at her carefully. "There was only one thing I could do. It was a danger to the world. A secret like that is terrible. Think what could happen if it got into the wrong hands! Into the hands of a man like Sline!"

"Sline isn't a problem any more," she answered.

"There are many men like Sline. And that's why I destroyed it."

"You destroyed the memory cup?" She was surprised.

"I had to destroy it! I broke it into a thousand pieces! Nobody will ever know the secret of the Mepatecs. They're dead. And so is their secret."

Dr Roberts thought for a moment. She looked up at the clouds and then she looked at Orwell.

"Do you think it'll rain?" he asked her.

She smiled at him. "Perhaps. But it won't wash our memories away, will it?"

He smiled at her too and said, "No!" And they walked on happily along the river.

What is the right answer: **a**), **b**) or **c**)?

1 When did Dr Roberts hear about the memory cup for the first time?
a) She couldn't remember.
b) After she and Orwell left the bookshop and walked along the river.
c) When Orwell told her about it after she bought his book about the Mepatecs.

2 What did Orwell find when he went inside the mountain?
a) The memory cup with all its secrets.
b) A story about memory on a strange cup.
c) How someone destroyed the Mepatecs.

3 How did Dr Roberts first feel when Orwell told her he destroyed the cup?
a) happy
b) surprised
c) it is impossible to know

4 Why did Orwell destroy the cup?
a) He wanted to be the only person who knew the secret.
b) He was angry because it almost destroyed his memory when Sline used it.
c) He thought the secret was too dangerous.

1	2	3	4

This is the end of *The Lost Secret*. But it doesn't have to be the end of your use of the video or of the book. You will learn more each time you watch the video again, just by listening and watching. And you can use the book again. You can read the cartoons and the story parts, and you can use the Review pages for reference. Happy viewing and reading!

Focus One

yet/still

Find the right sentence for each picture.

a) Has the film finished yet?
b) Has your mother come yet?
c) Has the policeman gone yet?

1	**2**	**3**

Focus Two

has done/have done/did

Find the right sentence for each picture.

a) Yes, we've already met. Your wife introduced us.
b) She's already arrived. She came ten minutes ago.
c) No, I've already seen it. I saw it last week.

1	**2**	**3**

Focus Three

since/for

Find the missing word. Is it *for* or *since*?

It's 9 o'clock. Peter is outside the cinema. He has been waiting for his friend ___1___ 7 o'clock. He has been there ___2___ two hours.

It's October. Jane has worked in this office ___3___ February. She has worked there ___4___ eight months.

It's Saturday. Sam and Ruth are in Spain. They have been there ___5___ Monday. They have been there ___6___ five days.

1	2	3	4	5	6

Focus Four

Would you ______ please?

Find the right sentence for each picture.

a) Would you turn it down, please?
b) Would you fill in this form, please?
c) Would you help me with my case, please?

1	2	3

Unit 11

Review

Now you have finished *The Lost Secret.* Do these tests and see how much English you have learned!

1 Study these questions (1–10). Find the right answers (a–j).

1 How do you do?
2 What do you do?
3 What are you doing?
4 What do you like?
5 What would you like?
6 Would you fill in this form?
7 Did you fill in the form?
8 How long have you been here?
9 How long will you be here?
10 When are you leaving?

a) Italian and Chinese food.
b) Yes, of course. Have you got a pen?
c) In a few hours.
d) Cooking dinner.
e) Pleased to meet you.
f) Since last Thursday.
g) Spaghetti, please.
h) About four more weeks.
i) Yes. I gave it to your secretary.
j) I'm a teacher.

2 Find the words that don't belong.

1 sun cloud gold rain
2 pen glass bottle cup
3 look sleep see watch
4 girl woman father lady
5 funny destroy happy laugh
6 year month day next
7 hotel garage petrol car
8 river mountain balcony beach
9 government garden plant flower
10 voice conversation telephone picture

3 Complete these sentences.

1 I was in London ____________ a week last year.
2 I've been here ____________ last month.
3 I came here a month ____________ .
4 When will you do it? —I've ____________ done it.
5 Have you finished the book ____________ ?
6 No, I'm ____________ reading it.
7 I ____________ to study English, but I teach it now.
8 Do you ____________ a pen or a computer when you write?
9 I know we have met before, but I can't ____________ your name.
10 Is he still here? —No, he's ____________ to work.

Grammar Summary

This is a short summary of the most important verb forms from **The Lost Secret**, and a few other things. It is not a complete guide to all the grammar in the course.

1.1

I	**am**	
You They We	**are**	English. American. in London. from Brazil.
He She It	**is**	at the station. here.

- This is the *Present* tense of the verb **to be**.
- The Present is the tense we use when we talk about *now*, *today*, etc.
- When we speak, we usually use short forms: **I'm** . . . **You're** . . . **It's** . . . **They're** . . .

1.2

Am	**I**	ill?
Are	**you**	on the right train?
Is	**she**	a good dancer?

- We change the word order when we ask questions with **to be**.
- We put **am/is/are** in front of words like I, you, he/she, etc.

This is your ticket. **Is this** your ticket?
You are a doctor. **Are you** a doctor?

1.3

I	am		
He She It	is	**not**	English. Greek. hungry. in Rome.
You We They	are		here. there.

- We use **not** to make the negative form.
- When we speak, we usually say **I'm not** . . . She **isn't** (or She**'s not**) . . . You **aren't** (or You**'re not**) . . . etc.

2.1

I'm	**a**	doctor. teacher. policewoman.
	an	engineer. architect. archeologist.

- Notice that when we talk about people's jobs, we use the indefinite article (**a**/**an**).
- We use **a** with jobs that begin with consonants (b, c, d, f, etc).
- We use **an** with jobs that begin with vowels (a, e, i, o, u).
- We use **the** when we mean 'the only one':

the director of this clinic (there is only one director)
the President of the United States
the Queen of England

3.1

This **That**	is	a beef sandwich. your coffee. the train to Winchester.

- We use **this** for things that are near to us; for instance, when we are touching them or when they are in our hands.
- We use **that** for things that are not so near; for instance, when we can't touch them.

3.2

These **Those**	are	beef sandwiches. your suitcases. the things from his pockets.

- The word **these** is the plural form of **this**.
- The word **those** is the plural form of **that**.
- We use plural forms when we mean *more than one.*
- The plural form of most nouns (thing, sandwich, coffee, pocket, book, car) in English is . . . **s** or . . . **es** (things, sandwich**es**, coffee**s**, pocket**s**, book**s**, car**s**).
- A few nouns have different plural forms (not . . . es or . . . s):

a **man**	two **men**
a **woman**	three **women**
a **person**	four **people**
a **child**	five **children**.

4.1

It's	**here.**
	there.

- **Here** means 'the place where the speaker is' or 'a place so near that I can touch it'.
- **There** means 'a place not very near' or 'a little distance away'.
  For example, when you phone a friend, and the friend's mother or father answers, you say, 'Hello. Is Bill/Mary **there**?' and the friend's mother or father answers, 'No, he/she isn't **here**.'

4.2

Here	it is!
There	

- You can begin a sentence with **Here** when you have something in your hand and someone wants to see it. For example:

  Ticket collector Can I see your ticket, please?
  Passenger Yes. **Here** it is.

- You can begin sentences with **There** when you are pointing to something not very close. For example, in episode 1 (see page 5 of your book), Sabina points to the bridge and says, '**There** it is. **There**! See it?'

5.1

There	is a fly in my soup.
	are lots of nice things here.

- This is very different from 4.2. When we say, 'There's a telephone in the next room,' we mean, 'You can find a telephone in the next room.'

5.2

Is	**there**	a doctor here?
Are		any good restaurants here?

- Notice the question form. Again, we change only the word order.

5.3

There	**isn't**	a doctor here.
	aren't	many good restaurants here.

- This is the negative. Notice again that here and in 5.1 and 5.2 we use **is** with singular nouns (doctor, fly, etc.) and **are** with plural nouns.

6.1

I	am	
He / She / It	is	**leaving.** / **going.** / **working.** / **coming.**
You / We / They	are	

- This is called the *Present Progressive* or *Present Continuous* tense.
- This form has many different meanings in English. We can use it for the *future*, for something we have already planned:

  I'm leaving tomorrow.
  We're going to the theatre this Saturday.

  and we also use it for the *present*, when the thing we are talking about is *happening now*:

  Hurry up, George! The train **is leaving**.

- When we speak, we use the same weak forms that we use with *to be*:

  I'**m** listening.
  You'**re** sitting in my seat.
  We'**re going** now.

6.2

Is	he / she	**leaving**?
Are	you / they	

- This is the question form. Notice that we simply change the word order again; that is, we put **is**, **are** or **am** in front of it, he, she, they, etc:

The train is leaving.	**Is the train** leaving?
It's raining.	**Is it** raining?
You're listening.	**Are you** listening?

6.3

I	am	
He / She / It	is	**not** leaving.
You / We / They	are	

- This is the negative form of the Present Progressive.
- Notice that we again form the negative in the same way we do with *to be*. That is, we put **not** after am, is or are.
- The weak forms are the same, too. When we speak, we usually say: I'm **not** . . . ing He **isn't** . . . ing You **aren't** (or You'**re not**) . . . ing.

7.1

I He/She You/We They	**can**	swim. speak English. come on Tuesday.

- We use **can** to talk about *ability* and *possibility*. For example, **I can swim** (ability) and **I can come tomorrow** (it is possible for me to come tomorrow).
- We use **can** for all persons (I, you, she, etc).

7.2

Can	you she he I they	swim? speak English? come on Tuesday?

- Notice the change in word order for the question form.
- We use questions with **can** not only to talk about ability or possibility (**can** you swim/come tomorrow?) but also in other situations. For example:

  Excuse me. **Can** you tell me the way to Oxford Street?
  Can you tell me the time?
  I know you're busy, but **can** I see you for a few minutes?

7.3

I You We She He	**can't**	swim. speak English. come on Tuesday.

- This is the negative form. The full form is **cannot**, but when we speak, we usually say **can't**.

  I'm sorry, but I'm busy. I **can't** see you today.
  He **can't** remember anything!

8.1

I He/She You/We They	**should**	see a doctor. get a haircut. write to my mother. do this homework.

- We use **should** when we want to say 'It is better for you to do this.' For example, if a friend is ill, you can say, 'You really **should** see a doctor!' If you think the friend's hair is too long, you can also say, 'You **should** get a haircut.'

8.2

Should	I we she they	do this? buy it? leave now?

- We form questions with **should** in the same way we do with **can**. That is, **should** comes first and then I, you, we, etc:

  What **should** I do now?
  Where **should** I put this?

8.3

I You We He	**shouldn't**	give him the drug. ask so many questions. do it. smoke here.

- The full form of the negative is **should not**. But when people speak, they usually say **shouldn't**:

  You **shouldn't** give him the drug, Basil!

9.1

Subject	**Object**	**Possessive**
I	me	my
he	him	his
she	her	her
it	it	its
you	you	your
we	us	our
they	them	their

- These are called pronouns. Words like **I** are called subject pronouns. Subject pronouns tell us who does something:

  I'm coming.
  They're going.
- Notice the difference between subject pronouns (I, she, etc) and object pronouns (me, her). For example:

  I can see **her**. **She** can't see **me**.
  We can see **them**, but **they** can't see **us**.
- Words like **my** are possessive adjectives. We use them with nouns in sentences like these:

  This is **my** coffee. And this is **your** coffee.

9.2

	mine	
	his	
This pen – is it	**hers**	?
	yours	
	ours	
	theirs	

- Words like **mine** are possessive pronouns. They stand for another noun. In this example, **mine**, **his**, **yours** stands for **pen**. The speaker doesn't want to mention pen again.

10.1

	Harry**'s** ticket?
Where is	Alfredo**'s** restaurant?
	the professor**'s** car?

- This is the possessive **'s**. We add it to the end of a noun:

  man man**'s**
  professor professor**'s**

  or to a name:

  Harry Harry**'s**
  Alice Alice**'s**

  to show possession.

- When a name ends in **s**, we simply write an apostrophe (**'**) at the end:

  Charles Charles**'**
  Where is Dr Roberts**'** clinic?

11.1

I/You We/They	**live** in . . . **work** at . . . **come** from . . .
He She (It)	**lives** in . . . **works** at . . . **comes** from . . .

- This is called the *Present Simple* in English.
- Notice the **s** after the verb (live**s**, work**s**, etc) with she, he and it.
- Notice that with I, you, we, they there is no **s** at the end of the verb.
- We use the Present Simple to talk about things that are true now, but *not* to talk about things that are happening when we speak. For example, Sabina says:

  I **work** in a bookshop. I **sell** books.

  When she says these things, she is sitting in a plane, talking to the man next to her. She isn't working in a bookshop or selling books at that moment.

- You can use the Present Simple when you want to talk about *how often* things happen.

  I **usually** watch television in the evening.
  I **always** start work at nine.
  I **never** drink whisky.
  I **sometimes** go to the cinema on Saturday.

11.2

Where	**does**	he she	**live**? **work**?
	do	you they	**come from**?

- This is the question form of the Present Simple. Notice that we use **does** or **do** and then the *infinitive* form of the verb, but without **to**:

  She **works** in a shop.
  Does she **work** in a shop?
  They **live** in Oxford.
  Do they **live** in Oxford?

11.3

I/You We/They	**don't**	live in . . . work at . . .
He She (It)	**doesn't**	come from . . .

- This is the negative form of the Present Simple.
- The full form of **doesn't** is **does not**, and the full form of **don't** is **do not**.
- We often use these full forms when we write, but we don't use the full forms very often when we speak.

12.1

What are you doing?
What do you do?

- Compare the Present Progressive and the Present Simple.
- We can use the Present Progressive for things that are happening when we speak:

  One man **is walking** to the bridge. The other man **is watching** him.

- We can also use the Present Progressive to talk about plans:

  How **are you getting** to your hotel?

  Sabina says this (see unit 3, page 28) in the aeroplane. Her question really means 'How do you plan to get to your hotel?'

- We use the Present Simple to talk about habits, things that happen often or sometimes, but not things that are happening as we speak.

  I **work** in a bookshop. I **sell** books.

- Remember the question 'What do you do?' means 'What is your job?' The question 'What are you doing?' means 'What are you doing at this moment?'

13.1

I You We They	**have got**	long hair. blue eyes. a lot of money. a new car.
She He	**has got**	three children.

- We use **have got** and **has got** to talk about possession – about things that belong to us or other people (cars, money, etc) or about characteristics (dark hair, brown eyes, etc).
- When we speak, we usually say:
  I'**ve** got . . . You'**ve** got . . . We'**ve** got . . .
  or She'**s** got . . . He'**s** got . . .
  It'**s** got . . . .
- Notice that the **'s** here stands for **has** and not **is**.

13.2

Have	you they	**got**	any children? the time? a car?
Has	he she	**got**	a lot of money?

- This is the question form. Notice that here **have** or **has** comes first, then the subject pronoun (you, they, we, I, he, she, it) and then **got**.

13.3

I You We They	have**n't got**	a car. any money. your address. a job.
She He	has**n't got**	

- This is the negative form.
- The full forms are **have not got** and **has not got**. We use the full forms when we write, but not when we speak.

14.1

I/She He/It	**was**	in England ill at school	yesterday. last week. at five o'clock.
You/We They	**were**	here there	in 1988.

- This is the past form of **to be**.
- We use the past form when we are talking about some *definite time in the past* (yesterday, last week, at five o'clock this morning, in 1988, etc).

14.2

Where	**was**	she he	yesterday? last week?
	were	you they	at five o'clock? in 1988?

- When we ask questions with **was** or **were**, we change the word order, just as we do with **am**, **is**, **are**.

14.3

I/She He/It	**wasn't**	in England ill at school	yesterday. last week. at five o'clock.
You/We They	**weren't**	here there	in 1988.

- The negative form of **was** and **were** is like the negative form of **am**, **is**, **are**. That is, we use the word **not**.
- Here you see the *weak* forms. What do you think the *strong* forms are?

15.1

I We You He She They	**explained** that to her last week. **finished** work at nine yesterday. **phoned** him yesterday morning. **came** home very late that evening. **went** to the cinema last Friday. **did** a lot of work this morning.

- This is called the *Past Simple*. It is the form we use in English when we think of or mention a *definite time in the past* (last week, at nine o'clock, yesterday, last Friday, in 1988, etc).
- In English, we have *regular* and *irregular* forms of the Past Simple.

Regular past				**Irregular past**	
ask answer call destroy explain finish laugh	+**ed**	believe like love smile phone use	+**d**	begin go come do see break put give have	**began** **went** **came** **did** **saw** **broke** **put** **gave** **had**

- The regular past form ends in . . . **ed** or . . . **d**:
  explain+ed phone+d.
- Irregular forms change in different ways:
  come **came**
  go **went**
  do **did.**

15.2

Did	you	**explain** this	yesterday?
	they	**phone** me	last Friday?
	he	**come** here	last week?
	she	**go** to the park	

- This is the question form of the Past Simple.
- We form the question first with **did**, followed by I, you, he, it, etc and then the verb.
- Notice the form of the verb (**explain**, **finish**, **phone**, **come**, **go**, **do**, etc). This is the same form as we use after **can** or **does/do** – the infinitive without **to**.

15.3

I	**didn't**	**do**	much work.
We		**watch**	television.
Mary		**listen**	to the news.
They		**go**	to work.

- The negative form is like **can't do**, **shouldn't do**, **don't/doesn't do**. That is, first we use the negative (**didn't**) and then the infinitive without **to** (**go**, **come**, **watch**, **listen**).

can't	+	go
doesn't		finish
shouldn't		see
don't		watch
didn't		come
		play
		do

- Notice that **didn't** is again the weak form; that is, it is the form we use when we speak. When people write, they often use the full form, **did not**.

16.1

I'm	**going to**	**ask** you some questions.
We're		**help** you.
He's		**give** you a drug.

- This is one of the ways we talk about the *future* in English. You can use it most of the time, when you are talking about *intentions*.

  What **are you going to do** this evening?
  I'm not sure. Perhaps **I'm going to see a film**. Or perhaps **I'm going to watch** television.

- We use it to make *predictions* as well.

  I think **it's going to rain**.
  I think Liverpool **is going to win** again this Saturday.

16.2

Are	you	**going to**	**answer** them?
	they		**help** us?
Is	she		**take** it?
	he		

- This is the question form. Notice again the change in word order.

  It's going to rain. **Is it going to** rain?

16.3

I'm	**not**	going to	do it.
You	aren**'t**		help us.
They			answer them.
He	**isn't**		take the drug.
She			

- Notice how easy it is to make the negative form. And notice again that with **I'm** we always use the full form, **not**, and never the weak form, **n't**.
- With you, they, we, and she, he, it there is another weak form that you can use:

  You**'re not** going to see me again.
  It**'s not** going to rain.

17.1

I	**'ll**	help you.
We		answer the phone.
She		do it for you.

- This is another way of talking about the future.
- The full form of **'ll** is **will**.
- We use **will** or its short form **'ll** for all persons.
- Sometimes people also use **shall** with **I** and **we**:

  I **shall** be in London next week.

17.2

Will	you	come soon?
	they	be here tomorrow?
	she	

- This is the question form.
- There can be a very important difference in meaning between **will** and **going to**, particularly in questions. We often use **will** in questions to ask people to do something:

  Will you close the window, please?
  Will you help me?

- Questions like these have a very different meaning from 'Are you going to close the window?' or 'Are you going to help me?' The meaning here is not '*Please* close the window' or '*Please* help me' but 'Do you *intend* to close it?' and 'Do you *intend* to help me?'

17.3

I You He They	**won't**	do it again. tell anyone. be here tomorrow.

- In the negative form, we usually say **won't**. The full form is **will not**.
- You can use **won't** to *refuse* to do things:

  I **won't** pay the bill! It's too high!

  or, again, to *promise* things:

  I **won't** be late again. I promise!

18.1

I/You We/They He/She	**used to**	smoke. play tennis. live in Brazil.

- We use this form to talk about things which we *did more than once in the past*, but which we *don't do now.* For example, 'I used to smoke' means 'I don't smoke any more.'
- You can make questions with **did** or **didn't** + **use**:

  Didn't you **use** to live in New York?

- We make negative sentences in one of two ways, with **didn't**:

  I **didn't use** to like oranges when I was young (but I do now).

  or with **never**:

  You **never used** to smoke (but you do now).

19.1

I/We You/They	**have to**	leave now. go to work.
He/She	**has to**	finish this.

- This is one of the ways we talk about *necessity* in English.
- We form questions with **do** or **does** + **have to** and the negative form in this way:

Do	you we	**have to**	do this? go there? listen to this?
Does	he she		

I You	**don't**	**have to**	go to work tomorrow. do any work today. do this now.
He She	**doesn't**		

- Another way of talking about necessity is **must**. We use **must** for all persons with the plain form of the infinitive (**finish**, **do**, **find**, etc).

I/You We/They He/She	**must**	**finish** it. **do** this. **find** him.

- Questions with **must** are formed in the same way as with **can** and **should**:

  When **must you be** there?
  Why **must you say** these awful things?

20.1

I/You You/They	**want to**	speak to the boss. buy a new car.
He/She	**wants to**	leave tomorrow.

- In English, this is only one way of talking about what we want to do. It is very direct and not always polite to say **I want to** . . . .
- Compare it with this form. It is more polite:

21.1

I/You We/They He/She	**would like to**	watch TV. have lunch now. live in Rio.

- When we speak, we usually say **'d** and not **would**:

  I'd like to ask you something.

- Compare the question forms of **want** and **would like**:

  Do you **want** to see that film?
  Would you **like** to see that film?

  The second question (**Would** you **like** to . . . ?) is more polite.

- Notice that we form questions with **would like** in the same way we do with **have got**:

  You have got a car.
  Have you got a car?

  You would like to see . . .
  Would you like to see . . . ?

→

- Now compare the two negative forms.

I/You		do that.
We/They	**wouldn't like to**	be there.
He/She		see it.

I/You We/They	**don't**	**want to**	go there. do it.
He/She	**doesn't**		see it.

22.1	I/You We/They	**have**	**been** there **seen** it	before.
	He/She	**has**	**done** that	

- This is called the *Present Perfect.*
- In English, we use the Present Perfect with words like **before**, **yet**, **already**, **just**:

  I've seen that film **before**.
  I've already seen that film.
  Have you **seen** that film **yet**?
  The film **has just finished**.

- We *don't* use the Present Perfect in English to talk about things that happened at a definite time in the past. For example, with words like yesterday, last week, in 1988, we use the Past Simple.

  I **did** it **last week**.
  I **was** there in **1988**.
  I **came** here **at nine o'clock** this morning.

- When we speak, we often use the weak forms: I**'ve** done it. She**'s** seen it. They**'ve** just arrived.
- Notice again that the **'s** here is the weak form of **has** and not of **is**.
- Now look at the question form:

  You**'ve seen** that film before.
  Have you **seen** that film before?

  She**'s been** here before.
  Has she **been** here before?

- and also at the negative form:

I haven**'t** She has**n't**	been here done this seen it	before.

- Words like **done**, **been**, **seen** are called the *Participle* form. This is different from the Past Simple form of the verb. Compare the forms in the Verb List.

Verb List

This is a list of some of the most important verbs from **The Lost Secret**. Regular verbs are in *italics*. Most English verbs are regular, but the most common verbs are irregular.

Infinitive	**Present**	**Past Simple**	**Participle** have/has...
to be	am/are/is	was/were	been
to begin	begin/begins	began	begun
to bring	bring/brings	brought	brought
to buy	buy/buys	bought	bought
to come	come/comes	came	come
to do	do/does	did	done
to drop	*drop/drops*	*dropped*	*dropped*
to eat	eat/eats	ate	eaten
to fall	fall/falls	fell	fallen
to find	find/finds	found	found
to fly	fly/flies	flew	flown
to forget	forget/forgets	forgot	forgotten
to get	get/gets	got	got
to give	give/gives	gave	given
to go	go/goes	went	gone
to have	have/has	had	had
to know	know/knows	knew	known
to leave	leave/leaves	left	left
to make	make/makes	made	made
to meet	meet/meets	met	met
to phone	*phone/phones*	*phoned*	*phoned*
to put	put/puts	put	put
to read	read/reads	read	read
to run	run/runs	ran	run
to say	say/says	said	said
to see	see/sees	saw	seen
to speak	speak/speaks	spoke	spoken
to take	take/takes	took	taken
to tell	tell/tells	told	told
to think	think/thinks	thought	thought
to try	*try/tries*	*tried*	*tried*
to watch	*watch/watches*	*watched*	*watched*
to write	write/writes	wrote	written